MW00898675

POP-UP THEATRE

A COLLECTION
OF NEW, AWARDED AND PRODUCED
SMALL CAST SHORT COMEDIES
DESIGNED FOR YOUR ENTERTAINMENT

PAULLETTE MACDOUGAL

authorHOUSE®

AuthorHouse™
1663 Liberty Drive
Bloomington, IN 47403
www.authorhouse.com
Phone: 833-262-8899

Published by AuthorHouse 09/26/2020

ISBN: 978-1-7283-7233-4 (sc)
ISBN: 978-1-7283-7231-0 (hc)
ISBN: 978-1-7283-7232-7 (e)

Library of Congress Control Number: 2020916803

Print information available on the last page.

This book is printed on acid-free paper.

*

SMALL CAST PLAYS
IDEAL FOR LIVE THEATRE AT HOME
READERS' THEATRE
PARTY ENTERTAINMENT
CIVIC EVENTS
CONTESTS
SENIOR COMMUNITIES
VIRTUAL PERFORMANCES
*

ROYALTY FREE
(If no admission is charged)

ABOUT PAULLETTE'S POP-UP THEATRE

NEW, AWARDED, AND PRODUCED PLAYS

Laughter energizes both body and soul.
So laugh!
A lot.

In addition to being fully produced productions in theaters, these short, small-cast comedies have been successfully presented in community organizations, fund-raisers, senior communities, and as no-lines-to-learn *(but lots of laughs)* home party entertainment.

RECIPE FOR LIVE THEATRE AT HOME

Gather friends or family.
Give each actor a copy of this book.
Cast the character roles.
Cast one more person to read stage directions.
Color-code the lines to be spoken easily by each.
Cast yourself as director.
Let the the fun begin!

You may be surprised at the acting talent your friends possess.

Without a paying audience, you may produce these plays royalty-free. However, it would be kind of you to let me know where and when. Or send me a video. I'd like to hear from you.

Paullette MacDougal
Playwright

Contact Information: paullette.macdougal@gmail.com.

GRATITUDE

My husband, Frank, who has always supported my writing, and has lovingly kept our household running smoothly while I prepared this manuscript.

My family, especially our sons, Colin and Michael, and our dear grandchildren, Veronika, Hallie, Morgan, Calvin, and Justin, who light up my life.

Many people contributed to my playwriting through the years, hundreds of them: Producers, Actors, Directors, Costumers, Stage Crew, Tech people, Ushers, Musicians, and a multitude of Volunteers who helped get my plays onto the stage. To name a few: Joanne Scanlon and Pam Heller of The Summit Playhouse (NJ), Christi Moore of Scriptworks (Austin, TX), and my many friends at Paradox Players (Austin, TX).

Gifted teachers: Director Wesley Balk, Ph.D, The Minnesota Opera; Professor Frank Daniel, Ph.D, Columbia University; The Reverend Robert Corin Morris, Interweave Center (NJ).

Special thanks to Cartoonist Kevin Schreck (contact@kevinschreck.com).

Many friends helped with this manuscript. Here are a few: Ann Buran, Diana Wolfe, Tricia Morris, Sue Poullette, Ann Edwards, Susan Roberts, John Ruffley, Sherry Coombs, Bonnie Watkins, Martha Iglehart, Jo Virgil, Stacey Keeler MacDougal, Dr. Diane Hill, Donna Van Straten Remmert, Jose Cruz, Gilma Cruz, Analy Garcia. Thanks to all for many decades of supportive friendship.

Paullette MacDougal

OTHER PLAYS BY PAULLETTE MACDOUGAL

WAITING FOR MACARTHUR
SISTERS UNDER THE SKIN
THE EMPRESS OF THE LAUNDRY ROOM
WALTZING THE REAPER
THE LAST WALTZ (Australia)
WE DO WHAT WE MUST
CHICKEN *A LA* APHRODITE
SOLO FLIGHT
TWO HUSBANDS IN HEAVEN
LITTLEST BIG KID (with Donna Van Straten)
BACKTALK (with Joan Weimer, Ph.D.)
EUREKA! (with Charlotte Pomerantz)
CRAZY BETT
RIPENINGS I
RIPENINGS II

CONTENTS

CAST SIZES

HERE COMES THE GROOM 1m., 1f.
HELL'S BELLS AND BUCKETS OF BLOOD 1m., 1f.
THE REVELATION 1m., 1f.
TALKING TO HENRY 1m., 1f.
THE SOLID GRANITE ROULETTE WHEEL 1m., 1f.
IN THE PRESENCE OF THESE WITNESSES 1m., 1f.
FIRE IN THE BASEMENT 1m., 1f.
ONE GOOD MOMENT 1m., 1f.

"CHARMING *SHARDS OF LOVE:*

Authentically Mismatched Couplings"

Courtesy of Theatre Suburbia

Kathryn Marie Crissman and John Wright in *Shards of Love*

By <u>Jim J. Tommaney</u>, ***Houston Press***, Mon., Mar. 7, 2011

SHARDS OF LOVE

by Paullette MacDougal

*Eight Short Plays, which Together Comprise
an Evening's Entertainment*

CAST: Flexible. Two actors portray different characters in each vignette
(Actors may be of any race or ethnicity)

TIME The near-past.

SET Two exits, left and right. Simple set pieces, colorful, whimsical.

SYNOPSIS

Each of the stories in SHARDS OF LOVE has to do with difficulties with love, commitment, life transitions, and celebrations that happen within different decades of romantic relationships, to couples from their 20s to their 90s.

In national competition, **HERE COMES THE GROOM** *was a* **FINALIST** *in the* **SIX WOMEN FESTIVAL 2009, Colorado Springs, CO.**

SHARDS OF LOVE *was premiered by* **Paradox Players,** *Austin, TX. Subsequently, it was fully produced by* **Theatre Suburbia,** *Houston, TX. Individual plays have since been staged elsewhere.*

Paullette MacDougal

SHARDS OF LOVE

EIGHT SHORT PLAYS FOR TWO ACTORS

by Paullette MacDougal

The Tantalizing Twenties	*HERE COMES THE GROOM*	10 Minutes
The Tempestuous Thirties	*HELL'S BELLS AND BUCKETS OF BLOOD*	10 Minutes
The Furious Forties	*THE REVELATION*	9 Minutes
The Fractured Fifties	*TALKING TO HENRY*	6 Minutes
The Spunky Sixties	*THE SOLID GRANITE ROULETTE WHEEL*	12 Minutes
The Serious Seventies	*IN THE PRESENCE OF THESE WITNESSES*	12 Minutes
The Emboldened Eighties	*FIRE IN THE BASEMENT*	15 Minutes
The Nostalgic Nineties	*ONE GOOD MOMENT*	8 Minutes
Run times, approximate without intermission		82 Minutes

"Thanks again for this play. The audiences are loving it."
— Elvin Moriarty, President, Producer
Theatre Suburbia, Houston 2011

"There are deep insights in this play."
— Amber Babcock
Musical Theatre Director

"You will love it."
— Jim J. Tommaney
The Houston Press

HERE COMES THE GROOM

by Paulette MacDougal

CAST:

LARRY   The Groom, late 20s, handsome, a practical joker, has some growing up to do.

CHLOE   The unblushing Bride, mid-20s, beautiful, brash, more of a match for the Groom than he expected.

TIME: The recent past.

PLACE: The "Bride's Dressing Room" in a church

SET: A folding screen, two chairs, a small table, a religious symbol or rose window shadow.

COSTUMES:

CHLOE: A two-piece specially-designed traditional-appearing bridal gown with a fashionable, almost strapless bodice, with an easily removable flouncy, full white skirt.

LARRY: Traditional wedding formal wear

*Unbroken happiness is a bore: it should have
ups and downs.*
– Moliere

HERE COMES THE GROOM

by Paulette MacDougal

*(BEFORE RISE: Church organ, wedding
music, "Here Comes the Bride")*

*(In darkness we hear a loud feminine wail, followed
by sobs, then indecipherable curses)*

*(AT RISE we see CHLOE, in her bridal glory, impatiently
trying without success to attach a rabbit's foot to her garter)*

CHLOE *(screaming)* GERALDINE! GERALDINE! I NEED YOU!!!
GET IN HERE!!! GERALDINE!!! *(repeat ad lib)*

SOUND: a knock on the door)

LARRY *(off, in a high falsetto voice)* Yoo-Hoo...Chloe? Chloe?

CHLOE *(shouting)* GERALDINE! WHERE HAVE YOU BEEN?
I CAN'T GET MY RABBIT'S FOOT TO STAY ON! I NEED
ALL THE LUCK I CAN MUSTER TODAY! HOW COULD YOU
DESERT ME LIKE THIS! AS MAID OF HONOR, IT'S YOUR
JOB TO WAIT ON ME – ME, THE BRIDE! YOU'VE LEFT ME
HERE ALL BY MYSELF FOR –

(LARRY opens the door a crack)

LARRY. Chloe?...Chloe?...Chloe, my darling?

CHLOE. Who's there?...Oh. Larry?

LARRY. Yeah. I'm the groom, remember me – ?

CHLOE. You can't be in here! GET OUT! GET OUT!

(CHLOE rushes to hide behind a screen. LARRY enters with a bottle of champagne and two goblets. HE sets them on the table. HE sings merrily)

> HERE COMES THE BRIDE,
> FAIR, FAT AND WIDE,
> THERE GOES THE GROOM – Ta-Dah!!!

LARRY. Chloe, I've got to talk to you –

CHLOE *(screaming from behind screen)* You can't see me before the ceremony! Aunt Viola said it's bad luck! With six marriages, she ought to know! GO! GO! GO! Where's my Maid of – no, my <u>Matron</u> of Honor?

LARRY. Last time I saw your friend Geraldine, she was…up-chucking on the best man.

CHLOE *(yelling)* Oh, God, No! Where are the bridesmaids?

LARRY. They're in the cloak room, getting crocked. They don't want to come in here. They're afraid of you…after you yelled at them.

CHLOE *(peeking out)* I didn't mean to! I was so nervous because you weren't here yet. You are always late! Tell them I am calm now.

LARRY. Calm. Good. That's why they sent me, to calm you down. We've got to talk.

CHLOE. We can't talk now. You're supposed to be – Where are you supposed to be? Lining up by the altar, I think. Go! Before the bridal march starts.

LARRY. No bridal march. The organist went home. Come on out.

CHLOE. QUIT JOKING! AND GET OUT! We agreed we'd do the traditional thing! You are not supposed to see me first until the service. We promised Mother! Where is Mother? Is she seated?

LARRY. She's…in the emergency room.

CHLOE *(stepping out from the screen)* WHAT? MOTHER? IN THE EMERGENCY ROOM?

LARRY. No, she actually isn't, but your father called an ambulance, just in case.

CHLOE. Oh, my God! Why?

LARRY. That's what I want to talk to you about.

CHLOE. Is this another of your comedy routines? Larry! Tell me straight! No idiot jokes this time. What's happening!

LARRY. Sit down.

CHLOE. Why?

LARRY. Sit.

CHLOE. I'll stand, thank you. Were I to sit, the back of my dress would get wrinkled, and we all know that it's our backsides that the people see at a wedding, which is why I've got my hair up in this ridiculous two-hundred-dollar up-do, that pulls my face up sideways. Larry, what's going on? No baloney this time.

LARRY. O — kay…There isn't going to be a wedding.

CHLOE. What?

LARRY. What I said. The wedding's off.

CHLOE. I don't believe you.

LARRY. Have a drink.

CHLOE. This is another of your bad jokes, right?

LARRY *(crossing his heart with his left hand)* Serious.

CHLOE. Tell me this is a bad dream. Why?

LARRY. Because...I – I don't want to.

CHLOE. Ooooooooo............Where's Daddy? Daddy can fix this...

LARRY. Your father said I was doing the "courageous thing."

CHLOE. Sounds like my Dad.

LARRY. Then good ol' Bob shook my hand and told me he'd send me the bill for the wedding.

CHLOE. That's Daddy! Fix the finances and everything else will fall into place.

> *(SHE sinks into the chair, mewing a sorrowful moan)*

LARRY. Chloe? Are you all right?

CHLOE. Maybe.

LARRY. Here. Have some champagne.

> *(HE pours her a glass of champagne, which SHE downs in one swallow. HE pours her another and one for himself and sits)*

LARRY. I should have said this earlier, but we've hardly talked to each other lately. With your mother's hot flashes cremating me whenever the subject of our marriage came up –

CHLOE. Larry! Don't talk about Mother's –

LARRY. And your Uncle Duck insisting that I take that catechism class –

CHLOE. Larry! *(coughing, from interrupted champagne)* Don't –Don't – Don't call Father Donald a duck! It's a priest's job to – to do the right thing.

LARRY. Actually, today, in his black robe, today he looks more like a penguin...

(HE wobbles and flaps his arms like a penguin)

CHLOE. Larry. Get serious!

LARRY. Yeah. Well, sorry, I sort of let it slide.

CHLOE. You let what slide?

LARRY. Uh...Telling you...that it's off.

CHLOE. What's off?

LARRY. The wedding.

CHLOE. What? Do I understand? We're – You and I – are not getting married?

LARRY *(drinking solemnly)* Correct.

CHLOE (rising) WHAT? What are you telling me?...Exactly?

LARRY. I decided...that the time...for us...like today...isn't the right time.

CHLOE. When did you decide this?

LARRY. A while ago…

CHLOE. You mean – You knew all this time, and…You let me go on… believing…trusting… fooling myself…planning…*(sobbing)* Picking out…our perfect china pattern!…and writing all those thank you notes in advance, because I wanted everything perfect today.

> *(SHE beats on him with the bouquet)*

Perfect! Perfect! Perfect! Damn you, Larry! I think I hate you! I do! I hate you! I hate you!

LARRY. Good. That will make it easier.

CHLOE. Make what easier?

LARRY. We've got things to decide. Like where we're going to live. Our apartment was my apartment first. I'd like to keep the apart—

CHLOE. Wait! Slow down! You just wrecked my wedding and now you are dumping me out on the street?

> *(SHE throws things at him as THEY slowly circle the stage. HE acrobatically manages to avoid being hit)*

CHLOE. You vile, hateful, evil creature, you! You are the meanest, most heartless – How could I have ever thought of marrying you? I must have been out of my mind! But wait! I think some measure of sanity is arriving. Yes! I need the Shopping Cure, that's what! Shopping is candy for the wounded heart. Shopping is medicine for the splintered soul…

> *(SHE aims to club LARRY with champagne bottle. HE grabs the bottle)*

CHLOE. And shopping is…a sweet, sweet balm that represses murderous impulses…Wait! Do I understand correctly? It's you who doesn't want to marry...me? Perfect me? Why? Tell me why? Is it because of the tattoo on my left breast? With another guy's name on it?

LARRY. No, not that...

CHLOE. It's my religion. You don't like my religion. You were always prejudiced against –

LARRY. No...

CHLOE. My cooking. You hate my cooking.

LARRY. No...

CHLOE. You don't like the way I make love.

LARRY. No, not that...

CHLOE. I spend too much money...

LARRY. You do, but no, not that.

CHLOE. It's because of the silicone in my boobs, isn't it?

LARRY. *(shocked)* You have silicone – there?

CHLOE. You're more naïve than I thought. What is it then?

LARRY. Oh, I don't know.

CHLOE. Oh, I know....You found out about Steve, didn't you?...

LARRY. What about Steve?

CHLOE. *(obviously lying)* Steve and I...had a little...fling... Here. Have a drink.

LARRY. Steve? My best man? When?

11

CHLOE. Let's see…When was it?…One of those times when you were drunk! Maybe it was after our engagement party!

LARRY. That can't be true!

CHLOE. I did! He did! We did! Ha-Ha-Ha. And I'm glad, you wretched, horrible man!

(SHE drinks more champagne)

LARRY. I don't believe it. You're just saying that to hurt me.

CHLOE. Why would I want to hurt you? Just because you're cruel! Inconsiderate!

(SHE threatens to whack him with a religious object)

You have humiliated me in front of everyone I know! I won't be able to face anyone, ever again!

(SHE tears up instead)

LARRY. Chloe. Settle down. I knew it already. Steve told me –

CHLOE. He told you – that? It isn't even true! I made it up! No! He made it up! The dirty toad! What scum you have for a friend!

LARRY. And you for a made-up lover? Huh? Is there something else you want to confess before we go in there and get married?

CHLOE. But you said – What about the organist? Mother?

LARRY. I told them we need some "private time." A new tradition. Private time for the happy couple replaces "can't-let-the-groom-see-the-bride-before-the-ceremony." I thought this would be a good time to get everything out on the table, no secrets, no hidden agendas, no lies –

CHLOE. *(hurt, mad, sobbing)* So you staged this ugly scene just to manipulate me, to make me confess things that didn't even happen! This has to be the most outrageous, most despicable, fugliest thing you've pulled yet! You vile monster! You're a heartless, sadistic –

> *(Still sobbing, SHE throws the champagne bottle at him, missing)*
> *(SOUND: a loud, splintery crash ["Shards" of glass])*

Oh, no! I forgot! It's terrible bad luck to break something on a wedding day. Give me –

> *(SHE grabs both goblets, drains them, and tosses them both off stage)*
> *(SOUND: crash-crash)*

LARRY. What did you do that for?

CHLOE. Bad luck comes in threes.

LARRY. That was three.

CHLOE: Three? Oh, my god! You're right. Got to dispel it right away. Ooooooommmmmmmm.

> *(SHE cleanses her aura, making sweeping motions down her body)*

Whew! I'm safe now, and I'm going to be real adult about this, Larry. *(taking charge)* Instead of poisoning you, or running you over, or helping you drown, since you can't swim – you lily-livered pussy – I'm going to – I'm going to –

LARRY. What you're going to do, Chloe, is go in there and marry me.

CHLOE. Oh, no, I'm not! You said, "The wedding's off." There isn't going to be a wedding.

LARRY. Chloe, my love…Be reasonable.

CHLOE. Reasonable! Is your juvenile behavior reasonable?

LARRY. It was a joke, Chloe. Just a joke.

CHLOE. Some joke, you mutant! You Neanderthal! I wouldn't marry you if you had the last functioning male appendage in the Western Hemisphere!

>*(a thoughtful pause, then, with a phony gesture of gratitude)*

Larry, Larry, Larry. Thank you, Larry. You have enlightened me. Now I know what life with you would be like. Thank you, God, may I never set eyes on this man again.

>*(With deadpan expression, SHE extends her hand to LARRY)*

Goodbye, Larry.

>*(SHE turns to exit)*

LARRY. Wait a minute! You can't just – Where are you going?

CHLOE. I'm going shopping. Shopping is the cure for all disasters. This has been a mega-disaster. Or a mega-disaster narrowly avoided. Or maybe, a wretched-but-necessary, mega-blessing. Either way, I need the Shopping Cure. I desperately need the Shopping Cure! Right now! And I have –

>*(SHE pulls a credit card from her bra. SHE kisses the credit card, waves it)*

Voila! – our "Honeymoon Account" to do it with!

LARRY. No! You don't mean that! Chloe! Don't! Please! Give me that credit card! CHLOE!

(Laughing, SHE puts the card back into her bra. HE falls to his knees, begging. SHE slowly and deliberately unties the bow on her flouncy white skirt. Stepping out of the skirt SHE reveals her "shopping outfit:" tall white high-heeled boots, and very short white shorts)

CHLOE. *Au revoir,* my last and latest love... *Au revoir,* Larry. Au revoir...

(SHE throws a kiss at him. Pausing only momentarily in a rebellious, sexy stance, SHE sends LARRY an "I dare you!" gesture. SHE throws the skirt at him and exits determinedly to "go shopping")

(MUSIC: The organ swells into the traditional wedding entrance music "HERE COMES THE BRIDE")

(The LIGHTS fade on bewildered LARRY, who is sobbing as HE buries his head in the flouncy white bride's skirt)

END

HELL'S BELLS AND BUCKETS OF BLOOD

by Paullette MacDougal

CAST: JANIE   Thirty-something. Attractive, good figure. An animal lover.
She wears jeans, a tee shirt.

       HERBIE   Thirty-something. A hunter. Handsome. A big burly guy.
A woodsman in a full deer hunting outfit.

TIME: In the near-past and the near-future.

PLACE: Inside a modest home in rural deer hunting country.

SET: Box set with one door and several windows.

PROPS: A facsimile of a shotgun.

EFFECTS: Preparation for dropping paper hearts. *(See end of play)*

SYNOPSIS

It's deer season. Husband Herbie and his brothers are passionate hunters. Janie wants to protect every last Bambi. Even more than that, she desperately needs to protect her home from the bloody mess that butchering venison in her kitchen made last year. She uses her three best weapons: a prayer, a gun, and sex appeal.

HELL'S BELLS AND BUCKETS OF BLOOD

by Paulette MacDougal

*(AT RISE: JANIE kneels in an attitude of
prayer, a shotgun at her side)*

JANIE. You know, God, it's deer season again…I feel sooooooo guilty about what I did today. I ran out into the woods this morning, banging on my soup kettle, shouting, "Run, Bambi, run!"

Big mistake. I scared the whole herd right over to where Herbie and his murderous brothers were waiting. Bang! Bang! Bang! Bang! Bang! – Five dead Bambis. And all my fault…Leonard even thanked me. Offered me a tender tenderloin. Me, the vegetarian animal lover!

Actually, I'm lucky to be alive. After a four-beer and jerky breakfast, they'll shoot at anything that moves.

(SOUND: Loud rapping on the door)

JANIE *(calling)* Don't bother me now, Herbie. It's my prayer time. *(back to praying)* That's my problem today: Guilt. That brings up an interesting question, God. Do you have deer hunting in heaven?...I hope not.

> *(HERBIE is off-stage, looking in through a window. When he changes windows, JANIE aims that way)*

HERBIE *(off)* Hey, Foxy Lady, open the door!

JANIE. Uh-uh, Hot Dog Man.

> *(SOUND: banging on door, other impatient male voices)*

HERBIE *(off)* I can see you, Cupcake. I know that gun isn't loaded.

JANIE. Herbie, you Big Banana. You think your Little Chickadee doesn't know how to load a shot gun?

HERBIE *(off)* Come on, open up! The boys are waiting.

JANIE. I know. I can see Leonard's ugly ol' green pickup out back with dead things hanging all over it.

HERBIE *(off)* They're waiting to bring them in.

JANIE. Like last year? No. No. NOOOOOO!!!

HERBIE *(off)* I can't let the boys down...

JANIE. Tell your murderous brothers to go home and contaminate their own kitchens.

HERBIE *(off)* My brothers will each pay me $500 cash to cut up their deer carcasses.

JANIE. You told me already, "The meat processor costs lots more." Remember last year's deer butchering mess? After your brothers dragged those dead things through here, our home was a crime scene. AGHGHGHG!!! Blood! Buckets of blood! I vowed never again to allow –

HERBIE *(off)* Think what we could do with an extra $2000! Tax-free!

JANIE. I have thought. We would have to buy all new carpeting again, just like last year, since the blood stains didn't come off. That took most of the money. With the rest you bought a fancy new rifle. I don't see why we would repeat that stunt.

HERBIE *(off)* This year with the $2000 we also could buy you a new freezer, one of those really big ones. Nice place to keep your ice cream cold.

JANIE. And a ten-year's supply of smelly venison?

HERBIE *(off)* Or a big walk-in cooler. To put all those salads in when you have a party.

JANIE. My salads keeping company with your brother's bloody carcasses? No thanks.

> *(SOUND: Noise like a window opening. JANIE swings the gun that way)*

JANIE. I've got that window covered, too, you Big Chalupa! Don't try it...

HERBIE *(off)* You knew I was a hunter before you married me.

JANIE. Yes, I knew, but you described hunting as –
(SHE imitates Herbie's posture, holding gun vertically, like a cane)
"a gol'-darn, good, clean sport. Gettin' out in the air, trompin' around the woods." You made it sound like you were studying bird calls on the Appalachian Trail. Anyway, I thought you'd get over it.

HERBIE *(off)* Like I thought you'd get over being a vegetarian. You know what the word "Vegetarian" means? It's an obsolete Native American word meaning...

JANIE. I know. "Cain't. Aim. Straight." Not funny, Herbie. You tell me this every deer season.

HERBIE *(off)* I thought by now you'd appreciate a popular sport that also provides food. Girl, you looked beautiful today, running out in the woods, banging on that pan. You drove the herd right to our blind. I was so proud. I thought you'd changed your mind about hunting.

JANIE. How did I know your blind was over there? I was trying to save the deer.

HERBIE *(off)* In a war, that would be treason.

JANIE. In a war, the deer could shoot back. I heard that some of your other old hunting buddies thought they were back in the war zone. They got drunk the first day of deer season and started shooting at each other. You ought to be thankful you had to work that day.

Caused a big jam up at the hospital, it did. My friend Delores was in the last stages of labor, all by herself in the delivery room because the doctor was busy stitching up wounded hunters.

So Delores had to walk out to the lobby in her backless hospital gown to ask Barby the receptionist to deliver her bouncing baby boy. It was okay, though. Barby has birthed eight of her own. She knew what she was doing. Better than the doctor.

HERBIE *(off)* Janie, the boys are out of beer! Come on, Sweet Patootie! Put down the gun and open the door! At least throw us a six-pack!

(SOUND: banging on door. SHE aims at that door, yelling)

JANIE. STAY OUT! HERBIE, I'M WARNING YOU!

HERBIE *(off)* Have some mercy on us! It's cold out here!

JANIE. DOESN'T MATTER, YOU BIG HORNY GOAT! THIS KITCHEN IS MY SANCTUARY! I CANNOT COOK VEGETARIAN IN A BUTCHER SHOP! TAKE THOSE BLOODY THINGS DOWN TO THE MEAT PROCESSOR! GET YOUR BROTHERS PROCESSED WHILE YOU'RE THERE!

HERBIE *(off)* You're being so unreasonable.

JANIE. I MEAN IT, HERBIE! I'LL BE DAMNED IF– Sorry, God. I meant "I'll be darned." …

HERBIE *(off)* Janie, my love…Sweet heart…Love of my life…

JANIE. HERBIE! YOU AND YOUR BIG-FOOTED BROTHERS ARE NOT DRAGGING ANOTHER BLOODY CARCASS INTO THIS HOUSE! NOT INTO MY KITCHEN! NOT TODAY! NOT EVER!

> *(SHE pounds the floor with the butt of the gun. It goes off)*
> *(SOUND EFFECT: Shotgun fire, several times)*
> *(Terrified, SHE screams, drops the gun, opens the door)*

JANIE. Oh, my God! Herbie! Did I kill you? Are you bleeding? Ooo... Herbie! Are you all right?

> *(SOUND: Pickup trucks leaving rubber on the road, indicating that HERBIE's brothers hurriedly left. HERBIE peeks his head in the door)*

HERBIE. I'm all right. Are you? You scared the boys off – in a hurry. *(laughing)* I never saw my brothers move so fast.

JANIE. They took those poor bloody things with them?

> *(JANIE picks up the shotgun again)*

HERBIE. Yep. Five, all together. Including a beautiful eight-point buck. What a pity. Venison steaks. Venison sausage. Venison burgers...Janie, do you think we maybe have too many guns in this house? Want to talk about it?

JANIE. Herbie, do you want to come in?...

HERBIE. You bet I do, Doll, especially if you put the gun away. *(HERBIE enters)*

JANIE. You shouldn't have left your bird gun loaded.

HERBIE: You're right, I shouldn't have. Now I have to patch the ceiling.

JANIE. Herbie, I'm glad you're okay.

HERBIE. Me, too...Uh, Janie, you wouldn't have really, I mean, you wouldn't really have pulled that trigger on me, would you?

> *(SHE snuggles up to him sensuously)*
> *(LIGHTS: change to romantic lighting)*

JANIE. Umm...I think...I think...You'll have to wait 'til next deer season to find out...

HERBIE. Sorry, Honey. There won't be another deer season.

JANIE. What?

HERBIE. I accepted a new job. In Florida.

JANIE. They don't have deer hunting in Florida?

HERBIE. Better than that, I don't have any brothers there.

JANIE. Oh! Herbie! That's wonderful!

HERBIE. Here's the other part.

(HE opens his arms in a romantic invitation. JANIE throws her arms around him, hugging and kissing him as little red paper hearts drop like snowflakes from the ceiling. SHE stops suddenly)

JANIE. Wait a minute, Herbie. There's something I've got to do...

(SHE takes a prayerful pose)

Thank you, God, for fixing my problem...Amen.

END

THE REVELATION

by Paullette MacDougal

SYNOPSIS

Doug and Mary Ann are shopping for a house. Doug takes meticulous notes on his electronic device, calculating each house's merits and demerits. So far, he has found fatal flaws in each house they visited. In the laundry room of the "perfect house," Doug finally reveals why no house is good enough for him. This begins for them a more authentic relationship.

CAST:

MARY ANN –   40, a psychologist and wannabe mother.

DOUG –   40+, an methodical engineer and football fan, fearful of fatherhood.

TIME: The Present.

SET: Abstract approximation of a very large laundry room in a suburban house.

Maybe an ironing board, clothes line, clothes basket, or drying rack.

PROPS: Electronic device like phone or tablet.

Baby clothes, baby blanket.

THE REVELATION

by Paullette MacDougal

(MARY ANN enters expectantly, admiring the space. DOUG trails, checking off items)

MARY ANN. This is the biggest laundry room! Bigger than our first apartment! I'll put a bulletin board and family calendar here. Even the appliances convey! Great house. I like it.

DOUG. Appliances convey. Check.

MARY ANN. This house is so cozy. Don't you just adore it, Doug?

DOUG *(uninterested)* It's maybe one of the better ones.

MARY ANN. Out of how many? –

DOUG. Wait. I'm figuring...

MARY ANN. Eighty-seven, if we don't count the ones that were too expensive. This one just needs a little strong detergent here and there. *(admiring infant garments)* Aren't these adorable? This is sooooo cute! Look, Doug! Isn't this cute?

DOUG *(pounding the wall)* Sounds solid. Yep.

MARY ANN. New plumbing two years ago.

DOUG. Plumbing. Check.

MARY ANN. Realtor said the roof was new last year.

DOUG. Roof. Check.

MARY ANN. There's a nice workshop in the garage. (*caressing an infant garment*)

DOUG. Workshop. Check.

MARY ANN. An extra room by the front door. Perfect for my office.

DOUG. Office. Check.

MARY ANN. The garage has an extra bay. For your boat.

DOUG. Boat storage. Check.

MARY ANN. Look – a place to store your fishing rods.

DOUG. Storage. Check.

MARY ANN. Let's buy it before somebody else does. Let's buy it right now!

(SHE clutches a baby blanket passionately)

DOUG. Let's not move too fast…

MARY ANN. Doug, it sounds silly, but this is the house of my dreams!

DOUG. It's a big investment. We ought to check out the neighborhood.

MARY ANN. This neighborhood is *crème de le crème!* I want this house!

DOUG. I think we ought to look some more.

MARY ANN. We don't need to look more. This is it! After examining eighty-five houses…

DOUG. It's an older house. Let me figure…Things go wrong…

MARY ANN. Our agreed-upon minimum satisfaction criterium is eighty-seven percent. This house rates at...Look. Using your figures, Doug, this house is ninety-six-point-seven percent!

DOUG. Well, yes, but it doesn't have ...

MARY ANN. What doesn't it have?

DOUG. Well, quantitatively, it's almost perfect.

MARY ANN. Good. First thing we've agreed on for fifteen years. Let's make an offer. Now.

DOUG. I've got some unanswered questions.

MARY ANN. You examined the attic ceilings for leaks with a magnifying glass! You spent an hour down in the basement checking out the foundation! You've examined every inch of this house with a microscope. You still have questions? I love this house. Doug, what are you doing?

DOUG *(stepping off the room)* Measuring. Did you know that my foot is exactly twelve inches long? The same as Henry the Eighth. That's why twelve inches is called "a foot." Bet you didn't know that, did you?... Four, five, six...Yes! This might work...if we could put a big refrigerator right over there. Real handy.

MARY ANN. There's a nice refrigerator in the kitchen.

DOUG. There's room here for a nice big sofa to stretch out on. *(stepping off again)* Six, seven...Better yet, there's room for two small sofas. Don't like to watch football alone.

MARY ANN. You're going to watch football in the laundry room?

DOUG. Don't need a laundry room. Home theater. Entertainment center over there.

MARY ANN. Laundry is one of life's necessities. There's a den off the dining room for TV.

DOUG. I know how you women are about dens. You will decorate it all nicey-nice, put in all them fancy doo-dads, and turn it into a friggin' needle point studio where you can't even put your feet up. Mary Ann, this will be my room. All this stuff has to go, of course.

MARY ANN. And where will we do the laundry? Or isn't there any laundry in your psychological orientation?

DOUG. We could put a double decker washer-dryer combo in your office closet.

MARY ANN. Laundry in my office closet? A client is tearfully pouring out her life story and you will traipse through with dirty laundry?

DOUG. Who said I'd traipse through?

MARY ANN. Have you forgotten our agreement? You do the laundry, I vacuum. That's how we save money for the new house. You got the best part of the deal. No, we will move the washer and dryer to that end of the room, build a partition here, and make this side the nursery.

DOUG. The nursery? Mary Ann, is there something you haven't told me? Mary Ann, are you – ?

MARY ANN. We agreed, didn't we? We move into a house, then we'd – we'd have a –

DOUG. Sure, we agreed, but later, we meant later.

MARY ANN. This is later.

DOUG. I don't think we should rush into this.

MARY ANN. Doug, how long have we been married?

DOUG. Fifteen years, yesterday.

MARY ANN. That's what I mean! Fifteen years. This huge, beautiful laundry room reminds me that I am – I am – of a certain age – No! I am at a crucial age! And I am not a mother! I don't want to end up barren – fallow – dried up and lonely – longing for a – (*gesturing "baby"*)

DOUG. Could we talk about this later?

MARY ANN. Later? LATER! Doug, it's always later! I'm tired of later. I want now!

DOUG. Mary Ann, don't get so excited. This is just a laundry room.

MARY ANN. Not JUST a laundry room. This is a revelation!

DOUG. A revelation? Like Moses? We walk into somebody's stinkin' laundry room and you get a revelation?

MARY ANN. It wasn't Moses. Paul had the revelation. Moses had the ten commandments. No, it was John. John had the revelation.

DOUG. I knew it! It was John.

MARY ANN. You thought it was Moses.

DOUG. Mary Ann, do we have to get into another argument now? Here?

MARY ANN. Here. Yes. Here. It all comes clear to me right here. Very clear.

DOUG. Are you trying to say you like this laundry room?

MARY ANN. This laundry room is perfect! A perfect symbol for what's wrong with our marriage.

DOUG. You don't love me? Because of a stranger's laundry room? Because of Moses? John?

MARY ANN. This no ordinary laundry room! Like Stone Henge and the Vatican, this is a sacred space! Here is where the epiphany struck. The ghost of Carl Jung dropped a bucket of truth serum on my head. Right now. Right here.

DOUG. Isn't that too many metaphors for one thought?

MARY ANN. Laundry room, I love you! It's in the laundry room, where people's dirty little secrets get pre-soaked, scrubbed clean, and inevitably denied...

DOUG. Mary Ann –

MARY ANN. Yes! Denied! This is where one's missing buttons get replaced... Here is where life's little wrinkles get smoothed out... and...

DOUG. Mary Ann –

MARY ANN. It's here, right here in this laundry room, where my blind spot met my insight. I suspected it before, but today my eyes were opened...

DOUG. Listen –

MARY ANN. I finally understand why no house is good enough. A laundry room is the hub of family life – if one has a family. You, Douglas Jones, never intended to start a family. Measuring every house, up and down, calculating square footage...pretending. That's what you've been doing! Pretending! Like a stage show! This makes our marriage a fiction! Doug, I'm leaving.

DOUG. You're leaving...?

MARY ANN. You, Doug. You. Leaving you. You can talk to my lawyer.

DOUG. You – you just, like that – all of a sudden –

MARY ANN. Goodbye, Doug.

(*MARY ANN exits. HE follows, pulls MARY ANN back on stage*)

DOUG. You can't! Mary Ann! You are right! Look at the figures! This is the perfect house! Mary Ann! Don't leave! Mary Ann! Let's talk. Right here. In what you called sacred space! Let's talk!

MARY ANN. What is there to say? It's all been said.

DOUG. You're the one who believes in talk therapy.

MARY ANN. You don't. You said that a hundred times.

DOUG. Maybe I changed my mind. Talk. Go ahead. Talk.

MARY ANN. Okay…I want a family. Not a nieces-and-nephews-type family. A children-type family. Our children. You want – What do you want, Doug?

DOUG. I want – I want you, Mary Ann.

MARY ANN. That's not enough. (*SHE begins to exit*)

DOUG. Wait! You think I haven't thought about it. I have. I've thought about it a lot. It's a big responsibility to have children, to bring them up right…

MARY ANN. It is.

DOUG. Do all the things for them they need…

MARY ANN. Uh-huh.

DOUG. Remember their birthdays…

MARY ANN. Uh-huh.

DOUG. And Christmas…And teach him how to pitch and hit a ball – even if it's a girl – and I think – I think…Mary Ann, I think I'm scared. Scared I won't do it right. My Dad didn't do it right, and if I become a father, I'd want to do it right, and –

MARY ANN. Doug –

DOUG. Oh, honey, I don't know…if I can…do it right…

MARY ANN. Doug – Doug, Honey, I didn't know…

(MARY ANN stares at DOUG, as though seeing him for the first time. THEY reach their hands toward each other. MARY ANN takes DOUG in her arms to comfort him affectionately, like he is a child)

DOUG. Oh, Doug…My baby…My poor baby…

(LIGHTS fade to black)

END

TALKING TO HENRY

A Short Tragic-Comedy

by Paullette MacDougal

SYNOPSIS

Bob and Linda, in alternating monologues, confide their problems to "Henry." They reveal that they have lost their ability to communicate.

CAST: LINDA, 50ish, pleasant, attractive, well-dressed, and well-proportioned.

BOB, her husband, same age, graying at the temples. A nice guy.

TIME: Now.

PLACE: The sense of a nice home. Abstract.

SET: Two identical chairs, one on each side of the stage, facing the audience.

(It works well if the actors' focus is straight forward at eye level, as though talking to an invisible person, like a pastor or counselor. In our productions, the actors imagined that the "being" they are talking to is sitting on a sofa directly in front of them.)

PRODUCTIONS

Vail Club 50 in Vail, CO, sponsored a production of this play in 2016 in its *Cocktails and Conversations Series.*

This play was presented at **Paradox Players,** Austin, TX, in 2016 in its Reader's Theatre production of *"UH-OH Amore! Fractured Tales from Cupid's Files,"* as well as in the full productions of **SHARDS OF LOVE.**

"Talking to Henry," played at several locations in Madison, WI, including the **Bartel Center, The Overture Center,** and in various living rooms across the country.

TALKING TO HENRY

by Paullette MacDougal

(At rise, LINDA, 50ish, enters, sits in a chair, facing "Henry" [the audience]. It seems that she's talking to a therapist or a dear friend)

LINDA. It's so frustrating, Henry! It's like he doesn't hear me. He doesn't care what I'm going through. Every night, I wake up hot, sweating. I throw off the covers. Then I'm cold, so I cover up. Over and over. All night. I hate it that Bob sleeps right through my suffering. I hate his sleeping! Last night – I knew he had an early meeting – but I was so mad, I woke him up. I did! I poked him until he woke up.

(gesturing, poke-poke-poke)

Yes, I know that was bad. I guess I was hoping he'd be mad, too, so we could have a really good argument. But no, he had the nerve to suggest we make love! When I'm hot and cold, drenched in sweat? He said he doesn't care if I'm sweaty! Just shows that I'm nothing but a sex object to him. He'd have sex with a sweaty fence post!

(LIGHTS go out on LINDA and come up on BOB, who enters, sits, talks as though to therapist or a dear friend. This pattern continues)

BOB. Is she gone, Henry? Aerobics? Yoga? Book club? How the hell does she find so many ways to avoid me? She's turned into somebody I don't know. She talks about plastic surgery. She thinks her chin dropped and that makes her nose too high.

I swear, Henry, her nose is right where it always was. That's not all. She was talking about a leg extension procedure that Japanese women do to become taller. She wants to be tall and skinny like those bony anorexic models. Who wants to cuddle up to a skeleton? If we still cuddled...

I wanted to have sex last night. It's been a long time. I wanted to. I wanted her! She said, "I'm feeling fat." Tell me, Henry, what does "feeling fat" have to do with sex? So I said, "Linda, I love your body." Do you know what she said, Henry? She said, "You're objectifying me again. I'm not an object. I'm me."

What in damnation does that mean, "Objectifying?" Then she said I ought to be more "differentiated." Goddamn feminist gobble-de-gook! I just can't please that woman.

LINDA. Maybe things would be different, if I were slender. Skinny women can get by with things like being sweaty. Bean Poles, like my aunt, or fourth cousin – whatever she was – out in Hollywood. She was a child star, played 12-year-olds until she was 24. She's too rich to get sweaty. Skinny bitches like her can let their roots show and people think it's the latest fashion.

BOB. I told her I like a woman with some heft on her. Wrong! I learned that heft is a dirty word. I think the whole point about a woman is softness and curves – in the right places, of course. Even now, Linda has her curves in the right places.

She's not fat. I know better than to use that word! She looks great in clothes – without clothes, too, but she doesn't think so. She's taken to dressing in the closet for God's sakes!

LINDA. If I didn't feel so fat and ugly and have this hot and cold thing all the time, I'd have an affair. It would serve him right. Well, I'd have to find someone blind, who has a temperature deficit...I want, no, I need someone who thinks I'm attractive, who is passionate about me. Me! Not just my female anatomy!

Is it a sin, Henry, to think about having an affair? Is it a sin? A mortal sin or venial sin? Which one? To just think about it? I don't think so. I hope not. I think about it all the time.

BOB. And varicose veins. Damn! Did I tell you about that big flap? She noticed a new varicose vein the other day and actually started crying. I'd seen an ad, so I bought her some Vitamin K cream, supposed to do something or other to veins. She threw it at me, screaming, "What are you telling me? You're repulsed by varicose veins? You hate my body?"

God knows, I just wanted to help. I'm a man of action, Henry. When I see a problem, I got to fix it. I feel so helpless...

LINDA. Bob's hair is silver. (*Or is going gray. Or is balding.*) I don't care. It doesn't make him less attractive. Fiftyish men become dignified. We women just get saggy. I hate saggy!

BOB. Yesterday, I told her she looked great in whatever it was she was wearing. She said, "Don't lie to me. I can tell when you're lying."

LINDA. One of the things I love about you, Henry, is that I can trust you. You will never repeat anything I say to you about Bob. I can count on that... (*at exit*) Henry, we'll just pretend we didn't have this little chat. (*SHE exits*)

BOB. Thanks for listening, Henry. You're the only one I can tell all this to.

(HE rises, takes a few steps, pauses)

I feel better already...

(HE removes a bright red dog leash from his pocket)

Come on, Henry.

(HE twirls the bright red dog leash)

Good boy, Henry. Let's go for a walk.

(LIGHTS slowly fade to black),

END

THE SOLID GRANITE ROULETTE WHEEL

by Paullette MacDougal

SYNOPSIS

After a long and not-so-happy marriage, merry widow Luella is looking for some excitement. To make up for lost time, she has purchased a motorcycle and plans to drive it to Alaska "by way of Hollywood." The ghost of her late husband, a betting man, tries to deter her. Their past differences and infidelities are revealed as they place a bet on the style and cost of his tombstone.

CAST:

LUELLA   Busty, athletic, bleached blonde, skirt too short, blouse too revealing. Altogether, she is dressed too young for a 60-something woman seeking adventure.

SAM   Luella's over-weight, pale and ghostly, dearly-departed working-class husband.

TIME: Now.

PLACE: Inside their garage in the Midwest somewhere.

SET PIECE: A real motorcycle, or a cardboard replica.

PROPS: A motorcycle saddle bag.
Tools.

> *"We see here a love that can survive the grave,*
> *yet without a trace of sentimentality."*
> – Jim J. Tommaney
> The Houston Press

THE SOLID GRANITE ROULETTE WHEEL

by Paullette MacDougal

(In blackout, LUELLA is heard howling loudly)

LUELLA. Ouch! Dammit! Owooo...

(At rise, LUELLA tries to attach a saddle bag to a motorcycle with a pliers, not successfully. The ghost of SAM, amused, watches)

SAM. Chipped your pretty fingernail?

LUELLA. Broke it. How long you gonna be hangin' around like this? Aren't you s'posed to be somewhere else? Heaven? Hell? Maybe just Purgatory?

SAM. Do you mind?

LUELLA. I had more privacy before you kicked the bucket.

SAM. Do I ever get in the way? Do I complain about your spending habits?

LUELLA. I can do what I want now.

SAM. Do I bother you? Do I object to your new bed mates?

LUELLA. If I have some, you're not s'posed to know about them.

SAM. There's lots I know, that I didn't know…before. This is Hell's punishment, having to know what we didn't want to know, back when we could have done something about it. Lulu, Baby, I get lonesome.

LUELLA. I told you not to eat french-fried bacon and three-egg cheese omelets for breakfast every day. Lonesome is what happens after massive heart attacks. You think I'm not lonesome? It's my money now and I'm gonna spend it my way.

SAM *(referencing the motorcycle)* What are you gonna do with that thing?

LUELLA. What do you think? Me and this here Harley are goin' to Alaska.

SAM. Alaska! Hah! You won't make it past the state line. Anyway, the Alcan Highway is narrow, curvy, a washboard of loose gravel. Only fit for trucks and bull dozers…

LUELLA. They paved it, Old Timer. Years ago. Actually, I'm going to Alaska by way of Hollywood. Gonna look up some friends from my glamorous movie days.

SAM. Let's face it, Luella. In Hollywood, you cleaned hotel rooms.

LUELLA. You think that's all I did? I had friends there – important people.

SAM. I don't care if you were bedding the whole Hollywood mafia. Your friends – if they were friends – have been dead for forty years.

LUELLA. Which is why I'm doing what I want, now that –

SAM. Now that I'm not around to tell you you can't?

LUELLA. You said it, not me.

SAM. You know, you gotta get a license.

LUELLA. That's what I'm going to do right now, practice for the road test.

SAM. Here? – In our garage?

> *(Or, if motorcycle is off stage, change to: "Here? – behind our house?")*

LUELLA. You think I'm going practice out there? Where the neighbors can see me?

SAM. You'll never pass.

LUELLA. If you'd leave me alone, I could concentrate.

SAM. I bet you don't even know how to start it.

LUELLA. You're a betting man, Sam. How much you want to put on it?

SAM. I don't have much left to play–

LUELLA. Hmmm…Maybe you do…Down in Arnie's memorial lot, I picked out the flashiest grave stone, all marble, Gothic arches, cute little cherubs on the top. But Arnie said it wasn't your type. Arnie said for ten grand more he could get you a custom sculpture. Real artistic. He suggested a replica of your Ford pickup, or your snow mobile, in solid red granite. "Somethin' ol' Sam really treasured." That was how Arnie put it. I gave it some thought. What was it that you really treasured? Then it was obvious: A life-sized replica of Eliza Mae Morton – nude!

> *(SHE gestures a shapely woman)*

SAM. Aw, Lulu. Don't bring that up.

LUELLA. I rejected that idea after Arnie pointed out that even in polished red granite, a voluptuous nude Eliza Mae Morton would look out-of-place in a cemetery.

SAM. Aw, Luelly...

LUELLA. Then Arnie said, "What else did ol' Sam really treasure?" That's when it came to me. A roulette wheel! A great big solid granite roulette wheel!

SAM. A roulette wheel! That's got class! I like it! Life's kind of a crap shoot anyway, isn't it?

LUELLA. Too expensive, though. So I ordered a little flat, highly polished rectangular thing.

SAM. The more I think about it, the more I like it! A big, red, solid granite roulette wheel!

LUELLA. Nope. Little, flat, highly polished rectangular.

SAM. Aw, Luelly, I like the roulette wheel! I want the roulette wheel!

LUELLA. So, Gamblin' Man, how much you wanna gamble? How about your tombstone! What do you say? I haven't closed the deal yet. Want to bet your tombstone?

SAM. Yeah. I'll bet my tombstone that you don't make it past the state line.

LUELLA. All right! If I come back alive – I get a new kitchen, and you get the little rectangle. If I don't come back alive, you get – *(sudden inspiration)* You get me! – For all eternity!

SAM. Sounds like I lose either way.

LUELLA. Is that what you think? Well. Here are the facts: You don't get to decide everything any more. Now go wherever it is that you're supposed to be, and let me practice. When I get back from Alaska – via Hollywood – after my new kitchen, I'll have $50,000 left for my next adventure – a long "Trojan" Caribbean cruise!

(OPTIONAL: SHE whips out a long chain of Trojans, preferably red packages taped together)

SAM. Aw, Luella...It wasn't my intention, you know, paying those insurance premiums all those years, for you to spend it foolishly on – *(indicating the motorcycle)*

LUELLA. You did have a certain lack of imagination when it came to enjoying living...

SAM. Dammit, woman! That money was earmarked to take care of you, in your old age.

LUELLA. And before I get to that old age, I'm gonna have some fun!

SAM. I wanted you to be comfortable.

LUELLA. Your idea of comfortable was going down to the casino. Here's mine...

SAM. I guess I don't need to worry. You'll never figure out how to run the thing.

LUELLA. You always underestimated me, Buster.

SAM. What if you break down on the road?

LUELLA. The dealer gave me a book. There's the starter. There's the gas tank. Oil goes there. Carburetor. Floating axle –

SAM. You know what nurses call motorcyclists? They call them "Our Best Organ Donors" You aren't even safe driving a car.

LUELLA. Safe! You were always playing it safe! See where playing it safe got you!

SAM. A woman alone, out on the highway: Highway bandits. Corrupt cops. Horny truck drivers. Or don't you plan to be alone? Lordy, Luella, who knows what you'll run into?

LUELLA. I can take care of myself. Remember out in Wyoming I shot, dressed out, and dragged that big buck down the mountain after you got a leg cramp?

SAM. That you did.

LUELLA. And I took care of Jasper, didn't I? *(SHE produces a small pistol)*

SAM. You shouldn't have done that.

LUELLA. I told him to get out of my bed. Then I told him again. When he didn't, well, I took care of the situation.

SAM. I don't expect you to be sleeping alone. I know you too well. But, Jasper. He was a pretty good guy...

LUELLA. When he was sober. And before he crawled in the window.

SAM. It wasn't as though he hadn't crawled through that window before. Geez, Luella, you could have asked him a third time, before you pulled the trigger.

LUELLA. Something I learned from forty years of living with you, Sam. Don't let a man walk all over you once, or he'll think he can walk all over you for a lifetime. My Grandmother Viola didn't let any man walk all over her.

45

SAM. Is that why she had six husbands?

LUELLA. Maybe she was restless.

SAM. I heard she once bedded Valentino.

LUELLA. She said Valentino was terrible in bed. Or was that Houdini? At least, she had an exciting life.

(SHE goes to work on the saddle bag in earnest)

I'm going to Alaska by way of Hollywood, and you can't stop me.

SAM. But who knows what could happen?

LUELLA. Worry, worry all you want. It will be more exciting than life here has been.

SAM. Aw, Lulie. I wasn't that bad, was I?

LUELLA. I'm not saying. Now let me work.

SAM. You gonna to wear that blonde wig? You look like a hooker.

LUELLA. How many sixty-five-year-old hookers do you know?

SAM. You ain't gonna make it back alive. Even if I win the bet, there'll be nobody left to order my big, red, beautiful, polished granite, roulette wheel tombstone!

LUELLA. Okay, Smarty Pants. I'll be fair. Before I leave for Alaska, I'll tell Janie, "If I don't come back alive, you buy the flashiest solid granite roulette wheel you can for your father's grave." But when I come back, Buster, it's the small, flat, polished rectangle. That's our bet!

SAM. You don't know what you're doing. Here. Let me do that.

LUELLA. No, thanks.

SAM. At least, use the right tool. You need a socket wrench to work those bolts...

LUELLA. Which one is that?

SAM. This one.

LUELLA *(working with the wrench)* You could have told me before...

SAM. It's not that I need some great big stone. But a monument means that somebody cared enough –

LUELLA. I cared, but you left me, Big Man –

(A tender moment. THEY almost embrace, but don't. LUELLA pulls away first)

LUELLA. Look. It's okay with me, you hangin' round the garage, helping me find the right gadget, or showing me how to check tire pressure and things. Sometimes, when you're haunting me in the house, that's nice, too, when I'm real lonesome. But, Sam, when I'm out on the highway with Harley here, that's my time, my space, my freedom. So stay outa my head, understand? It's just Harley and me, off on an adventure. Agreed?

SAM. Aw, Lulu, you're hurtin' my feelings.

LUELLA. Get outa here. I've got work to do.

(SHE goes back to work on the saddle bag)

SAM. You wouldn't do that to me, would you? A tiny, flat, rectangle thing?

LUELLA. Depends. If I have a good time, I might come home happy. Then I might want to honor you with that big, solid granite roulette wheel sculpture...Otherwise...

(SHE gets saddle bag secured. SHE admires her work)

Tah-Da! Saddle bag attached!

(Or, if motorcycle is off stage, use this line: "Tah-Da! Saddle bag ready to attach!" as SHE refers to the manual)

SAM. Lulie, I don't like to use those sappy words on Valentines, but I want you to come back with all your parts attached. That's more important to me than the tombstone. Understand?

(SAM points to the gauge, or to a picture in the manual)

You gotta watch this gauge, see? Don't forget to change the oil. You don't want a sudden freeze-up on the highway. You'd be a goner.

LUELLA. Is being a goner so bad?

SAM. Not so bad. Aw, Lu, you're right. It's your life now. Go on and live it. Live, I say! Hey, look here. You need these two buttons to start it. Press this one first, or you'll blow out the engine. Got it? This one, then that one. In that order. You gotta take care of yourself out there. Watch your speed. It's a twist-grip throttle control. Put your hands here. This is how you control the speed. That motion…Like that…Good. Now, start her up, my love. Let's see what this baby can do.

(HE backs into the shadows)

Drive careful, Lulie, drive careful…

(LIGHTS: Slow fade to black)
(SOUND: Motorcycle loudly revving up)

END

IN THE PRESENCE OF THESE WITNESSES

by Paullette MacDougal

SYNOPSIS

After Ted's retirement party, two aging former hippies mull over how they have spent the past 51 years together without benefit of matrimony.

CAST   EMILY 70+ The perfect hostess, attractive, pleasant, correct in every way.
She wears a party dress, now a little wrinkled.

TED 70+ The demeanor of a retired executive. He has his tie loosened, and his jacket removed.

SET: The essence of a patio after a large party. A bench or double seat settee. A small table. A trash can.

TIME   Late at night.

PROPS: Paper plates, napkins and utensils scattered about.
Liquor bottles.
An old-fashioned wedding dress with very full skirt.

SOUND: Off-stage voices.

IN THE PRESENCE OF THESE WITNESSES

by Paullette MacDougal

(In darkness, EMILY is bidding goodbye to guests after a party)

EMILY *(sweetly)* Thank you for coming to help us celebrate Ted's retirement...Drive carefully...Goodnight, dear friends...We love you... Come again soon...

> *(At rise, EMILY finishes waving, turns to TED, who sits on a lawn settee, liquor-bleary, staring at his empty glass.)*

EMILY *(angrily)* My God, Ted! I thought they'd never leave!

> *(EMILY cleans up used napkins and plastic ware)*

TED. Sit. Sit. Leave it.

EMILY. I can't just sit and look at this mess.

TED. Why'd they want to have my retirement party here, anyway?

EMILY. So they wouldn't have to clean up the mess?

TED. Leave it. They can come over in the morning and clean this place up.

EMILY. Donald is presiding at two weddings tomorrow. And Marcie doesn't clean. None of our D.I.L.s know how.

TED. D.I.L.s?

EMILY. Daughters-in-law. Our sons have a weakness for princesses without title or money. Still, it was a nice party.

TED. Too extravagant. We didn't need the ice sculpture.

EMILY. I loved the ice sculpture. A nice touch. And the *petit fours,* adorable!

TED. Is that what you call the little cakes with bugs on them?

EMILY. Not bugs! Replicas of your handmade fly fishing lures in Irish butter crème frosting! One of Marcy's better ideas.

TED. Cost a fortune. It will probably put us on Medicaid.

EMILY. To quote you, "Who are we saving it for?"

TED. Who indeed? Our girls are well set. Only Reverend Donald. He's poor as a church mouse – as is appropriate.

EMILY. It always amazes me. Two old hippies, with a clergyman in the family!

TED. We're rolling in respectability all right. Even the grandkids. Capitalists, all of them. Not a placard-carrier among them.

EMILY. Jody's a doctor. She's serving humanity.

TED. A plastic surgeon – boobs and schnozzolas! That's capitalism at its zenith.

EMILY. How long since you carried a placard? Or voted green? What about us? We gave in to the system. You were an accountant. That's not capitalism?

TED. It was work. Feed-the-family work. I'm glad to be done with it. It's perfect, though, how it turned out. Everybody's healthy and happy. Our sons seem happy with their Cinderellas. Yep. Everything's perfect.

EMILY. Not quite.

TED. Who's not happy?

EMILY. Me.

TED. What?

EMILY. Seeing everyone tonight – not the people from church – I mean our friends, Bill and Mary, my book group – they were all talking about how they celebrated their fiftieth wedding anniversaries, or how they're going to. They asked me about ours. They assumed, of course, since Donnie is fifty, that we already had our fiftieth. I hemmed and hawed. I blew my nose. Finally, I changed the subject. Dammit! Ted, I want to get married. I want to be an honest woman!

TED. You what? After fifty-one years? Married? Are you crazy? We've filed joint tax returns for, I don't know, ages. It's common law after so many years…

EMILY. Exactly. It's common. It makes me feel common and I don't feel married.

TED. You're not serious.

EMILY. I am. I want to do it the way we should have. I want to know you're committed to me. I want everyone to know.

TED. Haven't I been committed to you? "In sickness and in health…" I always stood by you… four babies, breast cancer, a hysterectomy, a dozens of fender-benders. What more do you want?

EMILY. We should have done it right away. Why didn't we?

TED. You tell me…

EMILY. At first, we were socialist. Then we were anti-government, anti-establishment. We were always anti-family –

TED. Only until Donny came. Then we suddenly <u>were</u> a family. You told your parents we got married in Vegas.

EMILY. My mother cried. But Dad was happy we left the commune.

TED. I'm still supposed to be grateful to him that he got me my first job.

EMILY. You told your boss we got married in Hawaii. *(sniffing sadly)* I've never been to Hawaii.

TED. Why'd we leave the commune, anyway? All those nubile young women. Why'd we leave?

EMILY. It was your amazing *rumori di tromba.*

TED. My what? Say it in English, please.

EMILY. *Rumori di tromba.* In Italian, it means, "sounds like a trumpet." Yours were something to behold. Like the brass section in the New York Philharmonic. It even embarrassed you.

TED. Oh, you mean my farts.

EMILY. Please. Your flatulence problem! You said if we had one more dinner of garbanzo beans, you were going to strangle Jason the cook. I thought you were serious.

TED. I was. That scumbag was feeding us beans and using the rest of the food budget for his cocaine habit. That's why I left.

EMILY. For me, it was when Donny got old enough to ask questions, like "Why don't we wear clothes," and "Which one's my daddy?"

TED. *(playfully)* I was never really sure about that. How'd we get a priest in this family? Is there something I should know? Before I change my will?

EMILY. Look in the mirror, Ted. He's got your eyebrows. Do you think he remembers those years? How do you think he'd take it, if he knew?

TED. Knew what? That he was conceived at a twenty-four-seven orgy with a bunch of stoned hippies?

EMILY. Were we hippies? We called ourselves the Beat Generation. Jack Kerouac. We were more intellectual than those Johnny-come-lately hippies. Cheap imitations, they were.

TED. I think we just liked to smoke and screw. Come on. Let's go to bed.

EMILY. We should have done it before.

TED. Before what? Gone to bed earlier? *(suggestively)* We can still make a night of it, a sort of party-after-the -party.

EMILY. No! What I'm talking about! Getting married. Making it official.

TED. What changed you, Emily? You were the most radical of everyone in the commune.

EMILY. After a few years, I came around to why people make a big deal about families. With children, things change. Commitment, that old fashioned word. It's something to celebrate. Something to proclaim to the world. Why didn't we?

TED. I suppose, after a while, it was plain inertia.

EMILY. We were hiding the fact that we weren't married, that's what it was. It was our secret.

TED. Our secret? Is that how you think about us? Living in sin? Nobody cares any about that any more. When did you start thinking about this, this wedding thing?

EMILY. Always. It took me a long time to get up the courage to say it: Ted, I want to get married.

TED. After four kids?

EMILY. I want to get married in church. Candles on the pews. A big cake with a bride and groom on the top. Vows. Got to have vows! White dress. The whole thing.

TED. You'd look ridiculous in a bride's white dress.

EMILY. Would I? Would I really, Ted? *(SHE starts to cry)*

TED. No-no-no. Not ridiculous. *(back-pedaling)* Inappropriate, maybe. Come on, girl, don't cry.

EMILY. I've got the dress. I've had it forever. Wait. *(SHE exits)*

TED. *(covering his eyes with his hand)* Oh God, Oh God, Oh God...

> *(EMILY enters with a large, billowing, out-of-date wedding dress)*

EMILY. See? I bought this right after Mary Lynn was born, as soon as I got my figure back. I've had it under our bed all these years. It still fits.

TED. How do you know it still fits?

EMILY. I try it on every year...on what I decided ought to be our anniversary. May first.
(SHE holds the dress in front of her, swaying romantically)
I thought that would be the best day. Spring flowers. May basket day.

TED. And International Workers' Day!

EMILY. That, too. So, what do you think?

TED. I think…it looks…like something your mother would have picked out.

EMILY *(sniffling)* Oh, Ted. We waited too long, didn't we? The time is past.

TED. You really want this thing, don't you? How about – what do they call it – "renewing your vows." They do that down at Donny's church, don't they?

EMILY. I don't want to renew vows never vowed in the first place. It would keep the lie going.

TED. The lie.

EMILY. Yes. That's what I feel. It's a lie. Us is a lie.

TED. Okay. Look, after fifty years, I don't feel like a lie, but if it means that much to you, I'll go along with it. I'll ask Donald if the church is free on May first. We'll have a big wedding. I'll proclaim my commitment from the rooftops! I'll tell everybody!

> *(HE runs to stage right and shouts "to the neighbors")*
> *(SOUND: Neighbors shout, "What's going on over there?"*
> *"Go to sleep." A dog starts barking, windows go up)*

TED. SAM AND MARTHA! IN THE PRESENCE OF THESE WITNESSES!
I LOVE EMILY AND I'M GOING TO TAKE THIS WOMAN TO LOVE AND CHERISH FOREVER UNTIL DEATH DO US PART. I DO! DO YOU HEAR ME? I DO! UNTIL DEATH DO US PART!

> *(HE runs the other way. EMILY follows him, dragging the dress)*

EMILY. Quiet, Ted! You will wake up the neighborhood!

> *(SOUND: Neighbors shouting: "Call the police." "Ted, are you drunk?" "Don't you know there's a noise ordinance?")*

TED. MARTY! GLORIA! NOW HEAR THIS! FOREVER AND EVER! EMILY DESERVES TO BE MARRIED! SHE DESERVES TO BE MARRIED IN THE CHURCH! IN WHITE! WITH ALL THE TRIMMINGS! IN FRONT OF ALL THE PEOPLE! I AM COMMITTED TO MARRY THIS WONDERFUL WOMAN, THE MOTHER OF MY CHILDREN, THE ONE I HAVE SPENT THE LAST FIFTY YEARS TAKING FOR GRANTED. UNTIL DEATH DO US PART! FOREVER AND EVER. AMEN.

(HE collapses into the patio settee, holding his heart)

EMILY. Ted! Should I call an ambulance?

TED *(catching his breath)* Just give me a minute. I'm not used to all this excitement. Emily, if you want a big wedding, you shall have a big wedding. I'll tell everybody we finally got around to it. I'll tell them we couldn't have a wedding earlier because we were too busy making love!

(EMILY gathers the white dress, sits down by TED, hugs him, and covers them both with the billowing white skirt like a blanket, with just their heads showing)

EMILY. Ted, I love you. I don't need a big wedding. I just needed to hear you say those words.

TED. You know I mean them…

EMILY. I know.

TED. Hey! How about a honeymoon? In Hawaii! Hell, why stop there? If we're going that far, we might as well keep going – an around-the-world tour! Who are we saving it for? How about it, Babe?

(THEY stay clinched under the dress, anticipating a kiss)

END OF PLAY

FIRE IN THE BASEMENT

by Paullette MacDougal

SYNOPSIS

An elderly couple plot to convince their son that they are capable of taking care of themselves without need of an assisted living residence. They try to show him how independent they are by cooking him a fabulous lunch. This spirals into an attempt by Carl to prove his virility by staging "auditory voyeurism."

CAST: CARL, 85, is a proud, blustering, retired plumber, with no experience in the kitchen, except to keep the drain clear. He refuses to take advice from any "authority," be it wife, or cookbook.

          GENEVIEVE, 83, has caviar tastes, but a baloney budget. She dreams of a different life. She coaches Carl from a cookbook because she has her broken right arm in sling.

          VOICE OF BOB, their conservative fifty-something son.

TIME   The near-past.

PLACE   The kitchenette of a run-down studio apartment.

SET   Movable counter with suggestion of an oven on upstage side. A real or fake dorm-type single-burner cooktop.
        (No working kitchen appliances are necessary)
One small table, two stools.

        One exit with a door.

FIRE IN THE BASEMENT

by Paullette MacDougal

(At rise, CARL, behind kitchen counter, casually plays with a garlic press. GENEVIEVE, her right arm in a sling, sits at the table with a cookbook and a glossy senior residence brochure)

GENEVIEVE. Carl, what time is it? Bob will be here in…

(SHE tries to look at her watch, but her arm isn't long enough)

Carl! Quit fiddling with that thing! This soufflé has to come out of the oven and be on the table minute Bob arrives. We don't want to give him an excuse to look into this poor excuse for a kitchen. It says…*(SHE puts on glasses and reads from cookbook)* "Whisk until mixture begins to thicken." So, whisk it.

CARL. With this thing?

GENEVIEVE. That's a spatula. The other thing is a whisk. Bob says Harmony Acres is nice.

CARL *(stirring)* I ain't goin' to no "high-class, congregate-care-assisted-living-residence." I don't need no congregate assistant poking around my private parts just because Bob thinks there's no juice left in this old man. He wants to put me out to pasture and get control of my estate, that's what!

GENEVIEVE. Like getting control of the hen house after the fox ate the chickens.

CARL. Woman, try to not get on my nerves while I'm concentrating.

GENEVIEVE. Look at this. Harmony Acres has white table cloths!

CARL. I don't care what color their table cloths, I ain't goin'! Just because there's snow on the roof – *(HE refers to his hair)* – don't mean there's no fire in the basement.

(HE references lower on his anatomy)

GENEVIEVE. Do tell….The brochure shows lots of activities. Pottery class, a gym. They even have dances.

CARL. They got categories there, did you know that? First you start out a GoGo.

(CARL imitates a GoGo dancer)

You think, Hey! This ain't so bad. Then you get a little run down, so they stuff you into SlowGo, and before you know it, you're a NoGo. That's the step before the morgue. I ain't goin'. What was I doing?

GENEVIEVE. You were whisking. We've got to get this done before Bob comes. Keep whisking.

CARL. I'm whisking, baby, I'm whisking. Couldn't we make something simple, like Beef Wellington or Lobster Thermodor?

GENEVIEVE. Sure. If our Social Security check had come. Better turn the heat up. Half the ingredients for Julie Child's Gruyere Cheese Soufflé are what we have in the house.

CARL. Where's the Gruyere?

GENEVIEVE. We're substituting Velveeta. Not real Velveeta, of course. The cheap brand. Bob says couples can room together at Harmony Acres. Roommates, like in college. That was fun.

CARL. It was only fun because I had to sneak into your dorm through the window. I think it's getting thick.

GENEVIEVE. Turn the heat down.

CARL. Up, down, up, down. Will you make up your mind?

(CARL bends to squint at the dial on the hot plate)

GENEVIEVE. Remember that comedy act we were working on? We should have gone on TV. We would be famous, like Bacall and Bogart. Lucy and Desi. Sonny and Cher. Everyone said we had chemistry.

CARL. We still do, Babe.

(CARL kisses her neck)

GENEVIEVE. Back off, Romeo. Go whisk the pot. Remember when we did that scene from Shakespeare?

CARL. When Othello choked me? He almost killed me.

GENEVIEVE. Your mistake was to be in bed with his Desdemona. Is it thick yet?

CARL. I didn't know they were a couple. Looks kind of pasty.

GENEVIEVE. Let me look. Add a little milk.

(CARL starts to pour from the container)

GENEVIEVE. STOP! Bring the pan. Let me look...This much. Now whisk it again. "Allow the mixture to cool slightly." Now, separate the eggs.

CARL *(putting two eggs in each hand)* Separated.

GENEVIEVE. That means, yolks in one bowl. Whites in the other.

(CARL looks like he's going to juggle the eggs)

GENEVIEVE. Careful with those eggs! That's all we've got to make lunch out of!...No! Gently tap the egg on the side of the bowl.

CARL. I know the principle. You just – (*the whole egg lands in the bowl*) Oh, shee--!

GENEVIEVE. Take a spoon and fish out the yolk.

CARL. How do you do this?

GENEVIEVE. Carefully. You do it carefully.

CARL (*struggling to spoon the yolk out*) Why can't we just make scrambled eggs?

GENEVIEVE. We have to prove we are capable in the kitchen.

CARL. All because Bob said, "You aren't eating properly?"

GENEVIEVE. "No. Because he said, you need somebody to look after you." This whole exercise is to prove to him that we are capable of looking after ourselves.

CARL. (*sniffing contemptuously*) A soufflé. Very capable.

GENEVIEVE. We'll be more capable when my cast comes off. Harmony Acres would be nice –

CARL. Got it! Separated!

GENEVIEVE. Good. A soufflé looks impressive, and feeds three nicely. Remember our "*Kiss Me, Kate?*"

CARL. Who could forget? The only time I got to give you a good spanking. Kinky old Shakespeare.

(*CARL sings, waltzing GENEVIEVE around the kitchen*)

BRUSH UP YOUR SHAKESPEARE,

DAH, DAH DEE DEE DEE...etc.

(Or some other song, permission required)

GENEVIEVE. You old fool! Look out! You'll break more than an egg!

(THEY BOTH collapse into chairs, laughing, winded)

GENEVIEVE. We're GoGo all right. GoGo take a nap. We should have gone to Hollywood when we had the energy. Everyone said we were naturals.

CARL. Your mother and your sister said. We were terrible.

GENEVIEVE. We sold out the last night.

CARL. Your father gave all your relatives free tickets. I don't judge a person by their relatives, but your relatives are so tight they'd watch a hog slaughterin' contest if the chow was free.

GENEVIEVE. Listen to me, Carl Miller! The best time to eat crow – and you know it – is while it's still warm...I'm waiting, Carl, I'm waiting...

CARL. Damn! I'm sorry, Genevieve. That was not the right thing to say.

GENEVIEVE. All right, then. Is it cool yet?

CARL. I guess so.

GENEVIEVE *(reading)* "Whisk in the yolks, Gruyere, prosciutto and chives..."

CARL. Prosciutto?

GENEVIEVE. That's ham. We don't have any. Just add the other stuff.

(CARL is ready to pour the egg whites into the batter)

GENEVIEVE. No! Stop! Not yet! You've got to beat them first! No! No! Use a different whisk! Not the one you used for the yolks or it won't poof up.

CARL. Holy balls of fire, woman! This is not Cordon Bleu!

GENEVIEVE. Slowly. In a circular motion. You're not chopping wood!

CARL. I ain't taken orders from anybody since I installed the bathrooms in the First Bank building forty-five years ago. After that, I called all the shots myself. I was damn good, too. Not good enough for your father, however.

GENEVIEVE. He thought you should have stayed in college.

CARL. Your father thought his daughter should have married royalty. Not a prince. That wouldn't have been good enough. A Czar maybe, or an Emperor.

GENEVIEVE. You never did like my family. It was like the Montagues and the Capulets.

CARL. The Montagues and the Capulets had class.

GENEVIEVE. I suppose the plumbing business is a class act?

CARL. Woman, you are getting under my skin again. Plumbing paid the bills so you could sit on your pretty little ass and carry on about going on the stage instead of dealing with water pipe leaks in filthy crawl spaces and shit up to my knees and irate customers who plugged up their toilets but need to take a fast crap. That's all I'm going to say.

GENEVIEVE. That was enough. Would you like to apologize again?...

CARL. Yes, Genevieve. I shouldn't have said that.

GENEVIEVE. You are right, as usual. Let me look...Now. The next step. "Fold in the whites, with a gentle motion so as not to deflate the volume." Gently is the operative word...gently...

(HE stirs the mixture none too gently. There are bowls all over)

GENEVIEVE. We could have had this lunch catered if you hadn't invested in that phony Ponzy scheme. Oh! Bob will be here any minute! Quick! Pour the batter into the soufflé pan! "Bake 18 minutes at 400 degrees until deep golden. Serve immediately." Quick! Put it in the oven!

CARL *(putting soufflé in "oven.")* There she is. All ready to "poof" up.

GENEVIEVE. Set the timer.

CARL. We'd have enough cash if you hadn't burned the house down. Twice. I've still got scars from the last one.

GENEVIEVE. Let me see your scars.

CARL. There.

GENEVIEVE. Here?

CARL. No, that one's when your dryer exploded. I ought to be able to enjoy retirement without coming home to land mines.

GENEVIEVE. You could have been nicer – civil at least – to that rich aunt of yours.

CARL. The one who had the lemonade funeral?

GENEVIEVE. Viola. You knew she was a teetotaler.

CARL. Being a dead teetotaler is no excuse to hold an Amish wake.

GENEVIEVE. Maybe she would have remembered you in her will, if you hadn't been drunk at her funeral!

CARL. I don't want no handouts! None from her, or anybody else!

(CARL throws up his hands in exasperation and sits at the table)

CARL. Genevieve. You sound like you aren't enjoying my retirement.

GENEVIEVE. It's lovely. Retirement is grand, wonderful, what I've always dreamed of.

CARL. I don't like the way you said that. What don't you like about it?

GENEVIEVE. Retirement is half the money and twice the husband.

CARL. Your turn.

GENEVIEVE. I'm sorry I said that.

CARL. But you are still thinking it.

GENEVIEVE. My thoughts are not entirely under my control...Nice décor at Harmony Acres.

CARL. A holding pen for the dried-up, given up, can't-get-it-up. I ain't goin'.

(SOUND: door opening off)

BOB *(off)* Hall-o! Anybody home!

GENEVIEVE. He's here!

CARL. Five minutes to go! It's a fault of our son never to be late.

GENEVIEVE. *(calling)* I'll be right there, Bob. Make yourself at home.

CARL. If he comes in here, he'll see how bare this kitchen is!

GENEVIEVE. He'll offer us money!

CARL. I won't take his money!

GENEVIEVE. Maybe, just a little loan to tide us over.

CARL. No! Not a cent! "Who controls the purse, controls the man." No.

GENEVIEVE. How you going to keep him out of here?

CARL. I'll make him a martini! He likes a twist of lemon!

(CARL finds dried-up old lemon)

GENEVIEVE. We don't have any gin!

CARL. That's what you think!

(From inside a pot full of kitchen utensils, CARL produces a small gin bottle, and from somewhere else, vermouth)

GENEVIEVE. What's it doing in there?

CARL. Hiding from you.

(SOUND: footsteps)

GENEVIEVE. He's coming this way!

CARL. Tell him you're not dressed.

GENEVIEVE *(calling)* I'm not dressed yet, Bob. Stay out there.

BOB *(off)* You're cooking? And you're not dressed?

CARL. Say you were interrupted.

GENEVIEVE. *(calling to BOB)* I was interrupted, Bob. *(whispering to CARL)* By what?

CARL. By the timer. The timer interrupted you…

> *(CARL is trying valiantly to cut a dried-up lemon. The lemon slips from his hand and drops. He crawls under the table to retrieve it, grumbling)*

DAMNATION!

GENEVIEVE *(to CARL)* Doesn't that sound kind of phony? *(to BOB)* I was getting dressed and the timer interrupted me. I'm making you a nice lunch.

BOB *(off)* I thought you broke your arm.

GENEVIEVE. *(calling)* Your father's helping. He's capable in the kitchen. You'd be surprised.

> *(CARL, cutting the lemon with brute force, cuts his finger, which bleeds profusely. HE wraps his hand in a towel and jumps around in pain)*

BOB *(off)* Yes, I would…be surprised.

GENEVIEVE *(calling)* Sit down and relax. We're fixing your favorite drink. How much longer?

CARL *(struggling with the olive jar)* The #@%$&* cover's stuck. Here. Hold the jar with your good hand.

> *(THEY struggle with the olive jar to no avail)*

BOB *(off)* How about if I come in there and help?

CARL *(calling to BOB as he pounds the cover)* No, no, son. You just relax. There's a new AARP magazine there. *(to GENEVIEVE, whispering)* Where's that thing you use to open jars?

GENEVIEVE. Maybe you had it last. Look around...Or...take the jar and the martini out there, ask Bob to open it, pluck out an olive, pop it in the glass and presto! A perfect martini!

CARL. That would show weakness. Can't do it.

GENEVIEVE. Stubborn old goat. Then just serve it without.

CARL. A martini without an olive? That's like a day without sunshine, a cupcake without frosting, a full moon without a woman in your arms, and a –

GENEVIEVE. Are you trying to tell me something about those trips to Vegas?

CARL. How can you say such a thing? Haven't you been my legal squeeze for fifty years?

GENEVIEVE. Sixty years – unless there's a decade missing, one where I considered myself married, and you didn't. I always wondered about the wild Seventies, open marriage, and all that.

> *(That's a subject CARL doesn't want to deal with. To avoid it, HE kisses GENEVIEVE, passionately.*

CARL. How could I look at anyone else, when you are my foxy lady, my kicky-wicky, my hot tamale, my red hot mama, my angel-faced baby doll, my –

GENEVIEVE *(pushing him away)* "A tale, told by an idiot, full of sound and fury, signifying nothing." Stop it, Carl! Bob's going to wonder what's going on.

CARL. Wonder what's going on! Yes! A brilliant idea! Something that will work even better than the soufflé! Oh, yes, yes, yes! You gotta go along with this, Genevieve.

GENEVIEVE. What does it involve?

CARL. Here. Sit down. Make yourself comfortable. Close your eyes. Now moan. Real authentic now, like you do.

GENEVIEVE. Like I do when, Carl -- ?

CARL. Like you do – when you're liking it.

GENEVIEVE. Liking what?

CARL. Just do it, Woman, moan.

> *(GENEVIEVE moans flatly)*

CARL. Not quite authentic…Remember that music appreciation course you dragged me to?

> *(CARL indicates the sounds he wants with wide musical gestures, like an orchestral conductor)*

1-2-3-Ready? Moan. Louder. What's it called? – *Crescendo! Molto Crescendo!*

GENEVIEVE *(moaning louder)* Oh! You mean like we're – *(suddenly SHE gets it)*

CARL. Right. You got it, Gen.

GENEVIEVE. It's been so long I can't remember how –

CARL. Sure you do. It's like riding a bicycle. 1-2-3- Now *forte!* Triple *forte*!

(CARL conducts. GENEVIEVE moans sensually)

BOB *(off)* Am I hearing what I think I'm hearing?

CARL *(calling)* A couple more minutes, son. Something we got to attend to here – Alone.

BOB *(off)* Shall I come back later?

CARL *(calling)* No, no, Bob. You wait right there. The main course is just moments away.

(to GENEVIEVE, waving his arms dramatically)

One more *forte*. Make this one *fortissimo!* Now, *Subito piano*. More like a purr. 1-2-3-

GENEVIEVE. I never purr.

CARL. Genevieve. Try. 1-2-3-

(GENEVIEVE meows loudly)

CARL. You're right. It was more like a meow. Good enough. Now that shriek. The one you do at the end. What do they call that?

GENEVIEVE. I never shrieked.

CARL. Oh, you shrieked all right. Real loud, too. *Sfortzando*! That's the word! One-Two-Three! The *sfortzando* shriek! 1-2-3- Do it now!

(GENEVIEVE shrieks. CARL laughs)

GENEVIEVE. Can I stop now?

(CARL kisses her hand affectionately)

CARL. Well done, Babe! That was your best performance yet!

(SHE realizes that CARL now knows that SHE's been "performing" for him all these years. She pretends to not understand)

GENEVIEVE. Performance? What do you mean? You know that I wouldn't pretend – I never –

CARL. I've never been able to please you, have I?

GENEVIEVE. Carl. You do please me…Sometimes…Not often…But…

CARL. You don't have to confess. I ain't that stupid. You're a good actress and I love you for it.

GENEVIEVE. (rising) Oh!... I've remember now! The old red purse!

CARL. What?

GENEVIEVE. The old red purse. For that jar thing.

CARL. Why the old red purse?

GENEVIEVE. That's where I put things I think I might forget that I forgot where I remembered to put them.

(SHE finds the rubber jar opener in the purse. CARL gets the jar opened, and puts two olives into the martini)

CARL. One, two. Look! A perfect martini! Beautiful!

(SOUND: the timer goes off)
(CARL removes the "soufflé" from the oven, sets it on the table proudly)

GENEVIEVE. And this is the most beautiful soufflé in the world!

(THEY high-five)

GENEVIEVE *(calling)* Bob, here we come! We're ready for our grand entrance!

BOB *(off)* Hey, wait. I think I have an appointment. I gotta go.

GENEVIEVE. No, wait! Let me explain – No, let your Father explain –

BOB *(off)* No – I don't want to know – I've heard – More than enough – Sounds like you two are okay living here. Martinis! Soufflés! And whatever else you were doing – I guess maybe you don't need assisted living yet. I'm out of here. Now you can finish – whatever it is you are doing.

> *(SOUND: Door closing. CARL laughs lustily)*

CARL. Bob will never again doubt his old man's virility, his prowess, or his ability to take care of himself. And his delightful, sexy mother.

GENEVIEVE. I think Bob's got the wrong idea about us...

CARL. Serves him right, spying on his parents' private life. Well. Ought not waste a perfect martini. My dear, will you join me?...Here's to voyeurism at its very best!

> *(CARL raises the glass and offers it to GENEVIEVE, who drinks. SHE hands it back and HE drinks. CARL gallantly pulls out a chair for GENEVIEVE, who sits. CARL offers her a fork)*

CARL. Soufflé, Genevieve, like so much of life, waits for no man.

GENEVIEVE *(waving the fork warningly)* No woman either, Carl. Don't you forget that!

> *(CARL sits. Forks poised, THEY are ready to attack the soufflé. LIGHTS slowly fade to black)*

END

ONE GOOD MOMENT

by Paullette MacDougal

SYNOPSIS

*Two elderly people sit on a bench outside a senior residence.
The woman is a loner. The man tries to make contact by sharing his
fantasy life and inviting the woman to dance. She resists his invitations
until they find a thread of connection.*

ONE GOOD MOMENT was finalist and First Alternate in
**AMERICAN THEATRE IN HIGHER EDUCATION
PLAYWRIGHT PROGRAM (ATHE).**

CAST:	BUD	In his 90s, spry for his years. He still has a sparkle in his eyes, a good sense of humor, and a soft place for a woman in his heart.
	CORA	She's in her 90s, but would never admit it. Once a beauty, her hard life has taken a toll.
TIME:		An autumn day in the near-past.
PLACE:		Outside a senior residence.
SETTING:		A bench, center stage.
COSTUMES:		Light jackets, scarves.

ONE GOOD MOMENT

by Paullette MacDougal

(At rise, Bud and Cora sit far apart on a long bench. She has a small "lap robe" over her knees. They both stare ahead, lost in their thoughts. He suddenly turns to her)

BUD. Hey! You want to dance?...Do you hear that music?

CORA. I don't hear anything.

BUD. The Good Humor Man is coming. Hear it?

CORA. There is no good humor in this place.

   (silence)

BUD. So. You want to dance?

CORA. No.

BUD. Why not?

CORA. 'Course I want to dance, Ol' Geezer. There's lots of things I want to do, but that doesn't mean I will do them.

BUD. The name's Bud. You don't like me?

CORA. I got no feelings either way on the question.

BUD. Do I smell bad?

CORA. I'm not close enough to know.

BUD. I'll come closer.

CORA. Don't bother.

(BUD moves to the other side of CORA)

BUD. This is my good ear. You want to talk?

CORA. No…You must be new.

BUD. New, huh? Which part of me would you call new?

CORA. If you aren't new here, you'd know I don't talk.

BUD. I saw you talking to that tree yesterday. You like talking to that tree better'n talking to me? Well, do you?

CORA. I wasn't talking.

BUD. You were. I saw you.

CORA. I wasn't. I was giving that tree a blessing.

BUD. Oh. You can give me a blessing. Right now.

(HE stands, faces her, opening his arms in a vulnerable gesture)

CORA. Wouldn't do any good, an old heathen like you.

BUD. How do you know that tree ain't an old heathen?

CORA. That's a dumb question. Anyway, I saw you talking to that fence over there.

BUD. Not dumber than talking to a tree.

(HE sits. Silence)

What did you tell that tree, in that blessing of yours?

CORA. It's not your business.

BUD. Maybe it is. Maybe I need a blessing, too.

CORA. I'm not taking any new clients.

BUD. These trees? They're your clients?

CORA. Sure. Haven't you noticed all these trees here are healthier than those over there?

BUD. I didn't notice.

CORA. These over here are my clients. And they've got more leaves on, over here.

BUD *(squinting)* Maybe so…

CORA. *(rising)* And they're got more birds in them! Can you hear the birds singing?

BUD. Maybe…No, I don't hear no birds singing.

CORA. Well, they're singing. They're singing their gratitude to the tree.

BUD. You're making it up.

CORA. I'm making what up? I tell you, they're singing their gratitude.

BUD. How do you know?

CORA. I just know.

BUD. You can't just know. There has to be some basis for your knowing. Like that dog over there, howling behind the fence. It's easy to know what he wants.

CORA. What does he want?

BUD. He wants somebody to come and tell him to sit or lie down or something. That's so he knows somebody cares about him. He'd even like somebody to tell him to shut up. So I go over there every day and tell him to shut up.

CORA. That's good.

BUD. What's good?

CORA. That you tell him.

BUD. You think so?

CORA. I know it. You gave him one good moment. I try to have one good moment every day. That's when bless the trees.

BUD. That's your good moment? Your best moment all day?

CORA. A tree is strong, rooted, permanent. Trees show peace and power. They make the air good. They give their lives to make our houses. So I go and thank them. They like being thanked.

BUD. "Only God can make a tree." I've heard that before.

CORA. Don't mock me. Of course only God can make a tree. You ever tried making one? And they branch out. They reach out to the sky and the birds. I like that.

BUD. You don't reach out.

CORA. I am not a tree...
(after a moment, CORA softens up a bit)
That's kind of special, though, about the dog, I mean.

BUD. What about it?

CORA. That you reach out to the dog. You got to walk 'way over there to give him his good moment. That's special.

BUD. Does that mean that I'm special?

CORA. I didn't say that.

BUD. A little special?

CORA. I didn't say that either.

BUD. Remember the Good Humor Man? When he came around in his truck, you could hear that rinky-dink song all over the neighborhood. Listen. Can you hear it?

(BUD tries to sing the tune, not well)

CORA. No.

BUD. Sure you can. All us kids would run home to get a dime for ice cream.

CORA. No, I don't remember.

BUD. Oh, you must.

CORA. We didn't have an extra dime for foolishness.

BUD. You could pretend that you had that dime, like you pretend about the trees and the birds.

CORA *(insulted, rising painfully)* I pretend? I'm going inside.

BUD. Wait. Wait. I didn't mean that. I meant, think, not pretend. You could <u>think</u> about having a dime. You know what a dime feels like, don't you?

CORA *(sitting back down, stiffly)* Of course.

BUD. Then think it. The dime. Right here between your fingers. Like this. Close your eyes. Feel the bumps in the silver...

(Silence as SHE sits with eyes closed)

BUD. And now you can think what flavor you want...Translate it into your brain: Vanilla, chocolate or strawberry...Which one do you choose?

CORA. *(Dreamily)* Strawberry...

BUD. Me, too. I can taste juicy chunks of strawberry. Sweet...Tart... The seeds still in them...

CORA. They used real berries in those days...

BUD....and real cream...

CORA....and real vanilla...

BUD....and you can feel the cool sweetness on your lips...

(HE leans closer, his face near hers. SHE suddenly jerks out of her trance)

CORA. What are you trying to pull? Are you one of those masher-types? All sweet-talking, nice-y-nice, like the Johnson boys, until they get you into their jalopy? There's lots of girls sorry they ever got into that forty Ford.

BUD. I didn't have a forty Ford... I had a thirty-nine, though.

CORA. Then you're just as bad.

BUD. But that was a good moment, wasn't it? I mean about the Good Humor Man?...Was it as good as talking to trees?

CORA. Maybe...

BUD. Come on, now. Tell the truth.

CORA. Okay, okay, it was a good moment.

BUD. So what brought you up to Alaska?

CORA. A man.

BUD. Cora, were you ever married?

CORA *(straining to remember)* Let me think...Probably...A least once... Maybe more...You?

BUD. Not that I recall...right now.

CORA *(teasing)* Those two women who came to visit you? I thought they were your daughters, the mousey one, and the half-naked phony blonde? Or are they your girlfriends?

BUD. Cora, are you jealous?

CORA. Certainly not!

    (CORA rises stiffly, as though to leave)

Some days, it's hard to get up, and then it's harder to get down.

BUD. How about sideways?

    (BUD mischievously moves his hips in a slightly sexual gesture.
    (CORA objects prudishly, although she actually"gets it")

CORA. What in tarnation is <u>that</u> supposed to mean?

    (SHE starts to leave)

BUD. Hey! Wait. You want to get married?

CORA. Me? Get Married? To you? No!

BUD. I'll give you some time to think about it. Not a lot, though. No use wasting time at our age.

CORA. I know what men are like. They are not like strawberry ice cream. They are like something else. They are like...Yes! Men are like caramel apples!

BUD. Caramel apples?

CORA. Right. All sweet and gooey on the outside. 'Til you get to the middle, then it's just another sour apple.

BUD. Aw, Cora. Maybe you just didn't have the right man.

CORA. I suppose you think you are "the right man."

BUD. No time like the present to find out.

> *(expansively, opening his arms)*

So, you want to dance now?

CORA *(pausing, while she thinks about it. SHE shrugs)* Might as well.

BUD. May I...?

> *(BUD takes her loosely into his arms)*
> *(SOUND: The Good Humor Music (permission required) fades up slowly. The music, formerly existing only in BUD's mind, is heard. BUD and CORA hold each other awkwardly, swaying in time to the music at first.*
>
> *Gradually they gain energy. They dance an old time dance, slowly, then faster, as the music segues into a peppier tune.*

END

> *(When producing the full-length play SHARDS OF LOVE with a full cast, the other actors may join Bud and Cora's dance for the CURTAIN CALL.)*

THE (ALMOST) PERFECT WISCONSIN WEDDING

by Paulette MacDougal

SYNOPSIS

It's the middle of the night, eleven hours after the "Perfect Wedding." Aimee the Bride is alone in her childhood bedroom beating on a pillow and howling hysterically.

The Groom has disappeared. Aimee has every reason to believe she has been jilted on her wedding night. She is consoled by Joleen, a bridesmaid, who offers tranquilizers, a huge martini, and a dubious prognosis.

CAST: AIMEE, 20, the maybe-jilted Bride.
JOLEEN, 22 the somewhat-consoling Bridesmaid.
JERRY, mid-twenties, the apparently absent groom.
TIMMY, a boy, Joleen's nephew.

(Actors may be of any race or ethnicity)

THE SCENE: The essence of the Bride's childhood bedroom in a modest home.

THE SET: One entrance.
One window, large enough to climb through.
A bed.

THE TIME: Night, in the recent past, while the "wedding reception-after-the-official-wedding reception" happens in the back yard.

(At the discretion of the director,
this short play may be substituted for
"Here Comes The Groom," as the opener
for the full-length SHARDS OF LOVE)

THE (ALMOST) PERFECT WISCONSIN WEDDING

by Paullette MacDougal

(At rise, AIMEE the BRIDE, in full wedding finery, is discovered face down on the bed sobbing, wailing, howling, and beating on a pillow. A tragic sight)

AIMEE. Rejected! *(sob)* Abandoned! *(sob!)* Deserted on my wedding night! He hates me! *(howl)* No! I hate him! *(snarl)* Embarrassing me... while all my parent's friends are out on the patio waiting to send the *(sniff-sniff)* perfect-perfect-perfect couple! *(Bawl)* Off to their perfect wedded life...After my *(wail)* perfect wedding! ...

(SHE rises, recalling the perfection)

Perfect flowers! Perfect music! Perfect lighting! Even the candles on the pews were perfect! Honey scented! Embedded with rose pedals! Custom made, pure beeswax! *(sob)* Cost Daddy a G-D fortune! Everything would be perfect now too, except for the absent groom! *(snarl)* I'll get even with him! I will! If it's the last thing I do!

(BRIDE twists her veil into a knot, throws it. SHE is still howling as JOLEEN, THE BRIDESMAID, enters. JOLEEN might be attractive if not wearing an ugly strangely colored bridesmaids' dress. SHE carries a very large fish bowl martini and calming medications: Demerol, Ambien, Oxycontin, and other potent tranquilizers)

JOLEEN. Aimee... Aimee, sweetie...Aimee! Calm down! Be quiet!

AIMEE. Get out! I don't want to see anybody!

JOLEEN. They can hear you downstairs. They can even hear you out on the back patio where your parent's friends are whoop-in' it up like the third time the Badgers won the Rose Bowl. They can probably hear you two counties away.

AIMEE. I don't care! Jerry promised we would leave for our honeymoon at 9:30, right after the church reception, so I could make a graceful exit, still looking beautiful. What time is it?

JOLEEN. Three thirty-seven. That's a.m.

AIMEE. AAAGH! I told Jerry I hate seeing a bride with her dress all rumpled up, the hem soiled, her satin shoes all scoffed, her mascara dripping –

(SHE looks into a mirror, howls)

AAAGH! MY MASCARA'S DRIPPED DOWN TO MY COLLAR BONES! GO AWAY!

(SHE throws herself down on the bed again)

JOLEEN. Aimee, you need help, and I'm here to help you. You've been away too long. You missed out on a lot of home town weddings. If you'd been here, you'd know more about the local customs. Here. I raided your parents' medicine chests. Which do you want? This one's good for anxiety. Or would you call this a panic attack?

AIMEE. My life is over! I'll be a 22-year-old divorcee, with the shortest marriage in history, doomed to be single forever, because the Catholic Church doesn't allow divorcees to remarry.

JOLEEN. Aimee – you don't get a divorce after a ten-hour marriage. You get an annulment.

AIMEE. Decades it takes the Vatican to annul, and by then I'll be old and *(sob)* undesirable…

JOLEEN. You're not Catholic anyway. He is, so it's his problem.

AIMEE. I'll kill him! *(sob)* Poison. *(sob)* No, not poison. Explosives... too messy. Ah! – The perfect weapon for the perfect revenge! I'll use Mother's butcher knife. The serrated one! On his tennis arm!

(AIMEE maliciously gestures sawing)

No! Dad's hunting knife! The really sharp one, right under his ears! And then, and then, and then, Dad's great big hedge clippers! I'll prune Jerry right where he'll remember forever why he deserved it. Yes! *(hoot)* I'll prune off his –

JOLEEN. Stop, Aimee! Stop! I want you to choose: Tranquilizers, pain killers, or is this triple martini time? What do you think? Maybe only half of an Ambien, plus this. *(The huge martini)* You'll be out for a glorious four hours. Here. I'll bite it in half for you.

AIMEE. Nothing. I want nothing. Just to be alone in my hopeless misery...

JOLEEN. Well, then, I'll drink it. Umm...This is the part I love about Wisconsin weddings.

(SHE takes a big swallow from the fish bowl, drinks periodically)

AIMEE. WHERE IS HE? THAT SCUMBAG I THOUGHT I WAS IN LOVE WITH?

JOLEEN. Well, let's figure it out. Calmly. When did you last see Jerry?

AIMEE. I couldn't find him at the reception, so Dad drove me home, so I could spend my wedding night in my childhood bedroom, ALONE! *(sob)* While everyone on my folks email list is down on the patio celebrating my PERFECT WEDDING! Dad said this party is his celebration, well-deserved, for getting me off his payroll. And now I'm not even off! *(Howls)*

JOLEEN. According to tradition, this party will go on 'til the rooster crows or 'til the old folks all pass out.

AIMEE. Where is that monster?

JOLEEN. Let's see. When I saw Jerry was at the reception, he was dancing the "Y.M.C.A." – You know – Y.M.C.A. Y.M.C.A. Y.M.C.A…
(JOLEEN sings a few bars, dancing about, arms waving)
That one. Really intellectual lyrics. Later, I saw him with his Madison buddies. It was about ten. So, I'd say – as an experienced Wisconsin bridesmaid – Never a bride – not yet anyway – I'd say that they probably took him to Moose Tavern for a night cap.

AIMEE. On our wedding night? Would they really? Did he go willingly?

JOLEEN. Not exactly willingly. It's a thing here. Anyway, he'd be rude not to go along with it. Last fling with the Buds. Sometimes they kidnap the bride, too. The reason they didn't kidnap you is the reason why I am the most in-demand, the most sought-after bridesmaid in the county. At Holly Jean's wedding I leveled one of the groomsmen, a two-fifty pound NFL dropout, with just one kick. To the right location. Like this.

(SHE demonstrates a karate kick, then drinks some more)

Because of me, Joanie Marie didn't get kidnapped either. Tonight I only had to deliver a couple of bloody noses. Kaiyah!

(SHE demonstrates a couple karate punches)

And, to really protect you, I flashed my sweet heat…

(SHE waves her skirt to reveal a small pistol strapped to her thigh)

And that, my dear sad bride, is why you didn't get kidnapped.

AIMEE. I suppose I should thank you, Joleen, but the bars close at one o'clock, it's now –

JOLEEN. It's now – later. Based on my extensive experience, I'd surmise that after they closed up Moose Tavern, Jerry probably found himself wandering a deserted country road, without phone, money, and most probably without pants...I hope they left him his shoes. Those back roads aren't paved. Pretty sharp gravel...

AIMEE. Oooooo...Jerry's poor bloody feet. Who are these Neanderthals?

JOLEEN. You know them.

AIMEE. Who are they? Which ones?

JOLEEN. Honey, you've been gone 'way too long. But Jerry's a runner, so, in spite of bloody feet, I expect that he got to your grandmother's by two, maybe two-fifteen...

AIMEE. Grandmother? What's Grandmother got to do with this?

JOLEEN. I heard your grandmother tell your dad that Jerry's car is locked in her garage.

AIMEE. Dad's in on this, too? I'll never forgive him.

JOLEEN. He said it will be a good story to tell your grandkids –

AIMEE *(sob)* Eternally single, I won't have grandkids –

JOLEEN. I might add that your grandmother supplied the poster paint –

AIMEE. Ooooo. Can you disown a grandmother?

JOLEEN. And also the tin cans tied on behind. We'll hear him driving up from a long way off...
Does Jerry know how to replace spark plugs?

AIMEE. Jerry *(sniff)* is totally non-mechanical.

JOLEEN *(offering sleeping pills)* Then, I'd recommend the whole Ambien. In the morning he can get a mechanic. No, tomorrow's Sunday. Might be Monday when you start your honeymoon.
Wait. I remember now. Timmy said that he knew all about spark plugs.

AIMEE. Spark plugs? Timmy is just a kid!

JOLEEN. Smart kid, Timmy. He was looking for a helmet so he could ride over to your grandmother's on your old bicycle to help Jerry with the spark plugs. I gave him a pair of slacks to take along, which I took out of your dad's closet in case Jerry's are – you know – gone.

AIMEE. Dad's pants are size fifty-two short! Tell me this is a nightmare!

JOLEEN. Better than nothing, especially if they've taken his underwear, too.

AIMEE. Everyone's against us! Oh, my poor Jerry!

JOLEEN. Does Jerry know your grandmother's garage door code?

AIMEE. I'm sure he doesn't.

JOLEEN. Good thing I gave Timmy a hair pin, too, in case he has to pick the lock. At Betty Lou's wedding they triple padlocked the automatic garage doors. Better take two sleeping pills.

AIMEE. No, thanks. I want to be awake to tell him what I think of his choice of groomsmen and their asinine pranks – I told him to ask my brothers instead of those Theta Chis!

JOLEEN. Those fraternity boys are from the Chicago. They didn't have a clue about Wisconsin weddings. Your brothers had to orchestrate the whole thing themselves.

AIMEE. My brothers? Bobby and Richie? I'll disown them, too! Oh, poor Jerry.

JOLEEN. They're just upholding an old Wisconsin wedding tradition. Really, Aimee, what you don't understand! They do this to show how much they love you, but they usually pull this stunt the night before the wedding. They were a little late this time. *(offering the martini fish bowl)* Here, take a sip. Fortify yourself to confront your brothers.

AIMEE. Dad? My brothers? Grandma? They all betrayed me?

> *(SHE throws herself down on the bed again, sobbing)*
> *(SOUND: rattle of cans on pavement)*

JOLEEN. Hear that?

> *(SHE sings, to tune of "Here Comes the Bride")*

"HERE COMES THE GROOM. IT'S DIE OR DOOM..."

TIMMY'S VOICE *(yelling, off)* Hey! Everybody! Jerry's here!

> *(SOUND: Car motor stopping)*

AIMEE. Timmy, too? Oh, my God! They're all in on it! Now I'm all alone in the world!

JOLEEN. Here, let me fix your makeup.

> *(SOUND: loud clunk, metal against siding)*

AIMEE. What was that?

JOLEEN. Sounds like your dad's ladder hitting the outside wall.

> *(SHE leans out the window)*

Yep. That's what it is. Good thing I left your suitcase in Jerry's car this afternoon. Here he comes. You're going to have to handle this on your own.

AIMEE. Don't tell me any more…

(JERRY appears at the window)

JERRY. Aimee? Are you here?

AIMEE. Jerry! Darling! My love! I was so worried!

(JERRY enters wearing a disheveled formal shirt, dangling bow tie, too-short over-sized brown slacks held up with a rope, his face smudged with grease. SHE runs into his arms. THEY kiss)

JERRY. We have about 30 seconds before your parents' well-oiled friends find their way to this side of the house. I'll climb back down to help Timmy steady the ladder. Then you come down. *(calling out window)* Timmy! Hold strong! I'm coming down!

AIMEE. You mean?...Me?…Climb down…the ladder? No. I'm scared of heights. I can't.

JERRY. Yes. You. Down the ladder. Now. You can do it, Babe. If you want us to get out of here before breakfast tomorrow, we've got to avoid the smashed well-wishers. Just pretend, my darling, that we are about to elope – which we should have done anyway.
(HE kisses her and quickly climbs out the window)

AIMEE. Jerry, I love you, but...

JERRY*(off)* I know. I love you, too. Come down the ladder. You can do it! One step at a time.

AIMEE. *(calling)* Catch me, Jerry. Catch me if I fall....

(AIMEE approaches the window with trepidation. Gathering up her voluminous skirts, climbs onto the window sill. Screaming, SHE disappears head first)

JERRY*(off)* Gotcha… Good going, Beautiful.

(JOLEEN peeks out of her hiding place, with almost empty fish bowl)
(SOUND: Car starting up, rattle of tin cans on pavement)

JOLEEN. Isn't that sweet? This is the part of Wisconsin weddings I like the best.

(SHE raises the fish bowl in a tipsy toasting gesture)

Many Happy Anniversaries, Lovebirds. Be fruitful and multiply!

(SHE calls down the window)

Timmy! You pint-sized scoundrel! You traitor! You promised not to fix the spark plugs until after sunrise!

(TIMMY enters through window)

TIMMY. I'm sorry, Aunt Joleen. I tried to do what you said. I even hid the tool box. But Jerry fixed his dad's classic car by himself. Fast, too!... Do I still get the twenty dollars?

(JOLEEN downs the rest of the martini)

END

JULIE'S BURGLAR

by PAULLETTE MACDOUGAL

WINNER - FIRST PLACE
Pandora's BoxTheatre Company
Escaping the Box
One Curtain Up Alley, Buffalo, NY

"Julie captures a burglar, and puts him in her employ,
[a plot] prime for "Saturday Night Live."
–Anthony Chase, Reviewer
Theatre Week

"It is a really nice showcase for actors
to show their range."
– Pam Cowan, Reviewer
Night and Day

"Julie's Burglar" is a wonderful script. A pleasure!
Ellen Opiela, Artistic Director
Pandora's Box Theatre Company

This short play was adapted by the author
from her much-acclaimed full-length farce,
THE EMPRESS OF THE LAUNDRY ROOM

JULIE'S BURGLAR

CAST
(In Order of Appearance)

BURGLAR   An attractive, but clumsy man with glasses, any age.

HOWIE   An inept executive-type in boxer shorts, who needs sleep.

JULIE   A small, pretty, fragile-looking woman, approximate age of Howie, with a surprising knowledge of martial arts.
She wears a very feminine nightgown.

(Actors may be of any race or ethnicity)

TIME: The near-past, late at night.
SET: A laundry room in a suburban house.
PROPS

An ironing board.
A clothes basket full of clothes.
Cleaning supplies, including toilet bowl cleaner with nozzle.
Assorted costume jewelry.
One pair of panty hose.
One beautiful pair of lacy women's panties.
A bath towel.
A flashlight.

OPTIONAL SET PIECES

A rack hung with elegant woman's clothing.
A facsimile of a mirror.
Facsimiles of a washer and a dryer.

JULIE'S BURGLAR

By PAULLETTE MACDOUGAL

(At rise, in semi-darkness, a clumsy BURGLAR enters, feeling his way in the dark. HE knocks over the ironing board, making a loud crash. HE swears under his breath)

JULIE *(screaming, off stage)* Howie, I heard something!

HOWIE *(off, sleepily)* Didn't hear nothin', Julie.

JULIE *(off)* I know I heard something. Howie, go look.

HOWIE *(off)* Go back to sleep.

JULIE *(off)* Howie, there's somebody in the laundry room! Get up and see.

(HOWIE, still half asleep, enters. BURGLAR holds up a towel to hide himself, not very well. Yawning sleepily, HOWIE turns on the light. HE doesn't see BURGLAR)

HOWIE. Nobody here, Julie. Maybe the ironing board fell down.

(HE sets the ironing board up)

JULIE *(off)* Check the locks, Howie.

HOWIE. You're imagining things, Julie. Go back to sleep.

(HOWIE turns off the light and exits. BURGLAR stumbles over the clothes basket, which dumps a heap of clothing on the floor. BURGLAR falls flat)

JULIE *(off, yelling)* Howie, I know there's somebody in the house! If you won't check it out, I will, dammit!

> *(BURGLAR burrows under heap of clothing on the floor as JULIE enters and turns on the overhead light.*
> *SHE spots his foot sticking out from the heap.*
>
> *SHE leaps onto the heap. BURGLAR groans painfully, his air knocked out. HE struggles to his feet.*
>
> *JULIE is fragile-looking, but she's fearless. SHE lands some hard karate chops on BURGLAR, who tries unsuccessfully to dodge them. Gaining the upper hand, JULIE winds his arm behind his back)*

BURGLAR. Ow! Don't do that! EEEEgh! You're killing me!

> *(JULIE shoves BURGLAR up against the wall, grabs a container of toilet bowl cleaner, pokes the nozzle into BURGLAR's back)*

JULIE. Hands up! Don't move or I'll shoot!

> *(BURGLAR believes it's a gun. Blubbering, he fearfully obeys)*

JULIE. Up against the wall! Hands up! Spread eagle!

BURGLAR. You knocked off my glasses – I can't see!

JULIE. Tough beans! I hate crooks. I'm deciding whether to kill you here or outside.

> *(SHE ties BURGLAR's hands behind him with a pair of panty hose)*

BURGLAR *(whining)* Oh, please, please, I'll leave, just let me go...

JULIE. Shut up, or you'll be picking your brains out of the sink.

(BURGLAR is helpless. She slips a pair of lacy bikini panties over his head, blinding him)

BURGLAR. You sure know how to embarrass a guy...

(JULIE frisks BURGLAR, finds jewelry in his pocket. SHE admires it dramatically)

BURGLAR. Cripes, Lady, I never hurt nobody. I'm just trying to make a living.

(BURGLAR whimpers as SHE pokes him again with the toilet bowl cleaner. A coward, this jewel thief seems to be in the wrong business)

JULIE. I'm feeling trigger happy. I'm warning you –

(JULIE finds more jewelry in burglar's socks)

BURGLAR. Please, lady, don't shoot me –

JULIE. One more move like that and I'll blast your gizzard into the washing machine. I'm deciding how to wipe you out without messing up my nice clean laundry room...This is Samantha Rayfield's emerald necklace! Burglar, you had a busy night!

(JULIE holds it up to her neck, looks into "mirror")

JULIE. I always thought it would look better on me.

HOWIE *(off)* Julie? You coming back to bed?

JULIE. *(To Howie)* In a minute, Sweetums.

(JULIE matches a necklace to an elegant dress hanging nearby)

Exquisite…Perfect! You steal nice ones, Buster. You've got good taste, I'll say that for you.

BURGLAR *(almost sobbing)* Just let me go, please. Just let me go…

JULIE. Cool your hooves! I got plans for you.

BURGLAR. Please, lady. I give to United Way. I donate blood…

JULIE. Button your lip, Robin Hood, or you'll find your pancreas in the lint catcher.

HOWIE *(off)* Anything wrong, Julie?

JULIE *(to Howie, demurely)* No, darling. Everything's nicely under control. Good night.

> *(BURGLAR whimpers as SHE shoves the toilet bowl cleaner nozzle into his back. again. SHE opens his wallet)*

JULIE. What kind of burglar are you, carrying your I.D.? I'll just keep this, so you'll remember to never come to this house again.

BURGLAR. Yes, ma'am, never, again. Not this house, not this street, not this neighborhood –

JULIE. Shut up! Here's what we're going to do. I'm keeping your driver's license…

BURGLAR. Please, not my driver's license! You know what you have to do to get a duplic–

JULIE. Shut up! I'm keeping your driver's license and – what's this? A letter from your probation officer? You're on probation?

BURGLAR. You ain't gonna blow the whistle on me, are you?

JULIE. Whistle? Man, I'm gonna sing them the whole opera! Oh, this is rich!

BURGLAR. Please, anything but that. Please, don't squeal on me! Please, anything.

JULIE. Anything? Did you say anything? Wait! I change my mind.

BURGLAR *(weakly)* You're gonna shoot me anyway?

JULIE. Maybe not. Let me think. I got it! We will be partners. Yes. Partners!

BURGLAR. Huh?

JULIE.Here's how it's going to be. I'll keep these documents, and you, dear visitor, will leave nice gifts for me under the geraniums in the big pot out front, let's say, on Sunday nights. Only quality stuff. Diamonds. Emeralds. You keep me happy, then perhaps I won't phone your probation officer. If I like the gifts, perhaps I will not press charges. If I am very happy, perhaps I will not say you assaulted and robbed me. Oh! I almost missed this one. You raped me, too! Remember, you slobbered your DNA all over my laundry.

BURGLAR. But I'm only a harmless burglar. I never hurt –

JULIE. Watch it, Bub! I don't like to be interrupted when I'm thinking. Let's see...where was I? Oh, yes, as I was saying, if you leave me a nice surprise every Sunday, and I will not say that you irreparably damaged my fragile psyche with your kinky demands. Understand? With your criminal record, along with my creativity, you'll probably only get life, unless I tell them that you also tortured my cat. If I tell them that, man, in this state, you'll fry. Understand?

BURGLAR. Yes, ma'am, yes, just let me –

JULIE. Shut up and listen. I want good stuff, no cheap costume junk. Under the geraniums out front, a good gift, or maybe two. Every Sunday night. Got that?

BURGLAR. I got it. Yes, M'am. A nice present –

JULIE. A very nice present.

BURGLAR. A very nice present. Every Sunday night...Oh, no, I'll have to work on weekends...

JULIE. Tough titty. Wait. You'll need these to find the good stuff for your next visit. Now get out of here. *(SHE places his glasses in his back pocket, leaving the panties on his head)*

BURGLAR. Like this? Don't, please, I'll be laughed at.

JULIE. That's the least of your troubles. Get moving! Follow the wall! Turn left now! Don't slam the door!....Bye bye, Mister Burglar.

(JULIE shoves BURGLAR out the door. SHE tries on the jewelry in a "mirror" and admires herself sensuously)

HOWIE *(off, sleepily)* Julie, you coming to bed?

JULIE. Right away, sweetie. Howie... Howie? Wake up! I'm feeling very rich....and suddenly, extremely...

(SHE wiggles sensuously, growls, like a tigress in heat)

very...extremely...romantic...Howie? How about it?

(JULIE exits with intent)

END

HONORS FOR JULIE'S BURGLAR

This short play, excerpted by the author
from the much-acclaimed full-length farce,
THE EMPRESS OF THE LAUNDRY ROOM
was produced at Theatre Suburbia, Houston, TX, 2019

The full-length script took these honors:

FINALIST, (Top three of 1700 entries)
Awarded a Public Reading
McLAREN COMEDY COMPETITION 2013
Midland, Texas

**FINALIST, BPP REVA SHINER
COMEDY COMPETITION 2019**
"Best of the Best," Top of the Finalist List
Bloomington Playwrights' Theatre
Bloomington, Indiana

WINNER - FIRST PRIZE
Awarded a Public Staged Reading
THE SUMMIT PLAYHOUSE PLAYWRITING COMPETITION
(former title, *L.I.N.T.)*
Summit, New Jersey

FINALIST (of 220 entries)
(former title, *THE LAUNDRY ROOM*)
BackDoor Community Theatre Competition
Wichita Falls, Texas

FINALIST (Top 4)
Oklahoma Community Theatre Association, Inc.
Oklahoma City, OK

BLOOMINGDALE'S ELEPHANTS

by Paullette MacDougal

"...the comedic frosting on the cake in this festival."
—Patricia Harvey, The Cheyenne Edition
May 2, 2008

The **Six Women New Play Festival** in Colorado Springs, CO, awarded **BLOOMINGDALE'S ELEPHANTS First Prize,** with a full production during the festival in 2008.

The **Six Women New Play Festival** amplified this honor when they chose this script as **one of the best plays they had produced in the previous ten years.** As a result, this play was honored again with a second full production at their 10th Anniversary Festival.

BLOOMINGDALE'S ELEPHANTS was featured at **Einstein's Bastards** in New York City in the "Seven Deadly Sins" Series. (Its sin was *Lust.*)

This play was given public readings at the **Camino Real Playhouse** in San Juan Capistrano, CA.

BLOOMINGDALE'S ELEPHANTS

by Paullette MacDougal

CAST

ALLISA   A pretty young woman, new on the job.

BABS   The Manager. She's worked in the gift wrap department for years.

MARK   A good-looking all-around guy, 30ish, about to be married.

(Actors may be of any race or ethnicity)

THE PLACE

The gift-wrap counter in a Bloomingdale's Department Store.

THE TIME

Wedding season, in the near-past.

BLOOMINGDALE'S ELEPHANTS

by Paulette MacDougal

(At rise, ALLISA and BABS are clearing the counter of scraps of wedding wrapping paper and ribbon)

BABS *(reading)* It says, "Product of Thailand." Do you notice anything weird about this new wedding paper?

ALLISA. You mean, beside those dopey little elephants around all the Bloomingdale's logos? Who'd want elephants on their wedding presents?

BABS. I mean, how it feels.

ALLISA *(feeling the paper)* I don't feel anything.

BABS. Feels funny. Sticky. Doesn't fold right. Somebody upstairs must like it. They never come down here. Not like Toys, or Cosmetics, where there's always a whoopee new promotion, with the executives strutting around with visiting celebrities. Nothing exciting ever happens in Gift Wrap. I wonder who chose this ugly stuff.

ALLISA. Somebody likes it. During your break a cute guy offered me $5 a sheet.

BABS. Five dollars a sheet? You didn't sell any, I hope.

ALLISA. Hell, no, I need this job. "No outside merchandise can be wrapped in Bloomies paper."

BABS. You got rid of him, then.

.

ALLISA. Not exactly. The guy was back in about ten minutes with a pair of jockey shorts and wanted them gift wrapped – in wedding paper!

I said, "You're giving jockey shorts for a wedding gift?" He said, "It's a present for me." Honest.

BABS. All kinds here. Wait. Did he look dangerous? Maybe we should call security.

ALLISA. Not dangerous. But you never can tell by appearanc – Oh, God, that's him! Over there! Headed this way. Probably with another pair of jockey shorts.

BABS. Let me take care of him. You go ahead and make up those ribbons.

    (MARK enters)

BABS. May I help you?

MARK. Yeah. Eh. I want to buy some paper. That one. The whole stack.

BABS. I'm sorry. Store policy –

MARK. Yeah, yeah, I know all that. How about a hundred dollars?

BABS. Sorry, I can't –

MARK. Two hundred? Five hundred? What's your price? A thousand?

BABS. Mister, I shouldn't be telling you this, but right down the mall there's a Hallmark store. They've got lots of real nice paper. Florals, plaids, –

MARK. I want this one! This friggin' one right here! Please call the manager.

BABS. I am the manager.

MARK *(pounding the counter)* If you're the manager, tell me what's so difficult about this? A minor transaction in a friggin' retail store?

BABS. Please. Calm down, or I'll have to call security.

ALLISA *(to BABS)* Babs, I don't think he's dangerous...

MARK. Look, lady, all I want is some paper. Does this store sell things? How about ten sheets?

BABS. Paper's not for sale.

MARK. But I've got to have it!

BABS. Yeah. Sure. I suppose your life depends on it.

MARK. My life, maybe. But my wedding does for sure. The invitations are out, the caterers hired. Hell, I just spent four hundred dollars on candles! I need this paper!

BABS. Your fiancée is partial to elephants?

MARK. No. She has excellent taste. A little bit inhibited, but –

ALLISA *(weakening, to BABS)* Oh, the wedding's all set. Babs, can't we just, this once –

BABS *(to ALLISA)* No. No. And No.

MARK *(to ALLISA)* You sell it to me, under the counter, sort of. Name your price.

BABS *(to ALLISA)* Don't you dare!

ALLISA. I'm – eh – curious. What would you do with all this paper, if I could sell it to you?

MARK. I – I don't want to say.

BABS. You're thinking of wrapping up cheap junk from Walmart and passing it off as Bloomingdale's, aren't you? You'll never get away with it. Uh-uh. Fraud! That's what it is! Fraud! They're real tough on fraud.

MARK. Uh-uh. Not fraud. Not me. Uh-uh.

BABS. Let's get down to brass tacks, Bub. I've been here fifteen years. Ain't nothing I can't wrap. Baby strollers, motor cycles, step ladders. What do you want to wrap?

MARK. I don't want to wrap anything. I want to – or rather – I want my fiancée to – Okay, this is sort of embarrassing –

ALLISA. You can tell us.

BABS. We won't laugh. We promise.

ALLISA. Come on, out with it. Maybe we can help you.

MARK. I – eh – eh – I want my fiancée to – to chew it.

    (ALLISA AND BABS both laugh hysterically)

ALLISA. Chew it? Wrapping paper?

BABS. This sticky stuff?

ALLISA. Like bubble gum?

BABS. Like chewing tobacco? *(to ALLISA, whispered)* Call security.

ALLISA. What's the number?

BABS *(to ALLISA)* The directory's in the drawer. I'll stall him.

    (ALLISA frantically searches a directory. She can't find the number)

BABS *(to MARK)* Eh, sir. You want her to chew it? My, that's interesting. Is your lady friend trying to break the chewing tobacco habit?

MARK. No, no, nothing like that. She's a classy gal. Pure. A little too pure...

BABS. Pure, huh? I'm taking a psychology course in night school. Is there something you need to talk out? I'm all ears.

MARK. I just need to buy some of that paper.

ALLISA *(to MARK)* What does it taste like? The paper.

MARK. Sort of – sort of – smoky. No, maybe a little like chocolate only more salty –

ALLISA *(licking the paper)* I do like chocolate. How did you discover this new taste sensation?

MARK. My fiancée and I – this is kind of embarrassing – we were just goofing around – we were opening early wedding gifts, and drinking champagne, and then we started tossing balls of wrapping paper at each other, and one thing lead to another –

ALLISA.You know, it does sound kind of romantic.

BABS. Let me get this straight, Mister. You were tossing paper, and then you decided to eat it?

MARK. No. We tossed it at each other, and then we started stuffing it into each other's mouths. You know, like wedding cake.

(BABS and ALLISA try unsuccessfully to stifle laughter)

MARK. I know. It's embarrassing.

ALLISA *(licking more paper)* I think it sounds like fun. So much fun you want to repeat it? With the same wrapping paper? I know. You're starting a tradition. I read in Bride Magazine that it's important for couples to start new traditions.

MARK. Is somebody else in charge here? Like Mr. Bloomingdale? Look, I'll just go find –

(MARK turns to leave)

ALLISA. Wait. You can't just leave us wondering --

BABS. Yeah. This is the most exciting thing that's happened in this department for fifteen years.

ALLISA. Come on. We won't laugh. Promise.

MARK *(to himself, turning away)* Jesus Christ! How do I get into these things?

ALLISA. Like chocolate. Here, Babs, Try it. It's good. Go ahead. Try it.

BABS. I don't know…

ALLISA. Go ahead, Babs. It tastes organic. *(reading)* "This innovative gift wrapping paper is part of a recycling effort an elephant conservation center in Thailand, which cares for forty elephants…" Sounds like a good charity.

BABS *(tasting the paper)* Not bad. For paper.

(BOTH chew the paper)

MARK. If I were you, I wouldn't – I mean, not here, I mean, just in case –

ALLISA. What's the matter? Your fiancée didn't die, did she? Is she in the hospital? Poisoned?

(SHE coyly unbuttons the top of her blouse)

MARK. Well, she was more – responsive. Hell, why am I talking to you about –

BABS and ALLISA. Go on.

MARK. She – uh – she's a New Englander. Very proper. Well-brought -up, you might say.

BABS. You mean she's a virgin? An icicle? They still exist. My psych professor said –

MARK. I don't want to talk about –

BABS. Frigid, right? Uh-huh. Your fiancée is frigid. I can always tell when a man ain't getting enough. They walk funny.

MARK. Do I walk funny?

BABS. Take a few steps and let me watch.

MARK *(almost taking a step)* Look, this is getting a little out of hand. I just want to –

ALLISA *(taking another piece)* Mmmm. I like it. Delicious. Fabulous. Cinnamon, I think.

MARK. I don't think you should do that –

ALLISA *(reading the label)* Looks okay to me…Some kind of international ecology project. "Our Elephant Preserve generates… electricity?… from natural gas. After the gas is extracted, the remaining material is made into — into decorative paper!

BABS *(relishing a delicacy)* Sort of like mushrooms. Or maybe like oysters.

MARK. Please, stop eating it. You don't know what could happ –

BABS. No, not oysters. Sort of like a man who's worked up a good sweat. My kind of man…

    (BABS stuffs a larger piece into her mouth and savors it)

ALLISA *(to MARK)* Nice eyes. Really beautiful eyes.

    (unbuttoning MARK'S shirt buttons)

You know, you're a rather good looking man.

    (BOTH WOMEN cuddle up to MARK suggestively)

BABS. I like a man who's got some weight *(or height)* on him. The bigger, the better.

ALLISA *(massaging his buttocks)* Great buns.

MARK. Hey! Cut it out!

BABS *(looking under his pants leg)* Got any tattoos?

MARK. Holy crap! It works the same on all of them –

BABS. You know, before a man settles down to married life, he should have an older woman. At least once. An experienced older woman.

    (BOTH women get more aggressive. BABS runs her hands up and down his bare chest. MARK tries to cover back up)

MARK. Oh, God, I've got to get out of here. Can I just have a couple sheets?

ALLISA. Did anyone ever tell you you're gorgeous?

BABS. That's how I like my men. Large and hard. Real hard.

MARK. No. Please, let go of me – Let go, I say! Help!

> *(Trying to escape, MARK trips and falls. The WOMEN each take one of MARK'S legs and drag him, struggling, behind the counter, out of sight as the struggle continues. Sounds of women growling sensuously and MARK resisting, ad lib, indicating that MARK is being ravished against his will. Some of MARK's clothing is tossed over the counter)*

MARK *(off)* Stop it now! Stop it I say! Let me go! Whoa! Ladies! Stop it!

> *(MARK crawls out from behind the counter, disheveled, partially naked. HE gets pulled back behind the counter, howling. HE crawls out again, stands, breaks into a run and exits. HE immediately enters, rushes to the counter, grabs a stack of paper and exits. BABS and ALLISA, dazed and sheepish, appear from behind the counter, straightening their clothing)*

BABS. Well. That was something.

ALLISA. That was. Something. I think. Yes. Something....Sort of embarrassing...

BABS. "Nothing exciting ever happens in gift wrap." Almost never...

ALLISA. Great buns...What do you think is in that paper?

BABS. What else did it say on the label?

ALLISA *(reading)* "Converting an energy by-product into wrapping paper helped solve the difficult problem of disposing of four thousand pounds per day of – ELEPHANT EXCREMENT."*

BOTH. Elephant shit! *(optional: dung)*

(BOTH WOMEN moan, scream, hold their stomachs and run off to hurl)

END

**Facts about the Elephant Conservation Center.
"News of the Weird" June 2001.*

THE POLITICS OF FISHING

by Paullette MacDougal

SYNOPSIS

Two middle-aged men, each recovering from a broken leg, meet outside a physical therapy clinic. Although they have nothing else in common, each has a desperate need to go fishing.

CAST:

CHARLIE: A plumber, talkative, confident, aggressive in a friendly way. He's lovable, which makes him safely short of obnoxious. He's older than Dexter.

DEXTER: A dentist, inhibited, socially insecure and very much an introvert.

(Actors may be of any race or ethnicity)

PLACE: A city street, outside a physical therapy clinic.
Later, at Charlie's fishing spot on a Wisconsin lake.

TIME: The recent past.

PROPS: Scene One:
A fishing Magazine, a marker.

Scene Two:
Two folding lawn chairs.
Two fishing poles, one tackle box.
One roll-on suitcase containing two beers, two short wooden dowels, two short hack saws, one cold pack containing beer and sandwiches.
Gummy worms.

Scene Three:
A rope hung with fake fish.

THE POLITICS OF FISHING

by Paullette MacDougal

Scene I – On the Street

(At rise: CHARLIE approaches DEXTER at a bus stop. BOTH wear leg casts and limp accordingly. DEXTER is reading a fishing magazine. HE isn't interested in talking, but CHARLIE persists)

CHARLIE. Has the ten-twenty bus come yet?

DEXTER *(without looking up)* No.

CHARLIE. You a fisherman?

DEXTER. Not really.

CHARLIE. So what's with this?

(CHARLIE snaps his finger on DEXTER'S fishing magazine)

DEXTER. My therapist said I need a hobby. I chose fishing.

(DEXTER turns back to his magazine)

CHARLIE. I knew it! Another member of the Fraternal Order of Anglers!

DEXTER *(back to his magazine)* I'm not interested in angling. I took a fishing course. Trout. End of explanation.

CHARLIE. At one of those fancy resorts up north? Where they lie around naked in the sauna and only pretend to go fishing? I read about those places.

DEXTER. I think I see the bus.

(DEXTER tries to extradite himself from the conversation)

CHARLIE. Fishing courses only catch suckers. Suckers. Get it? How many fifteen-hundred-dollar rods did you buy? And over-priced neoprene waders? Lures at two hundred a crack? Those fancy resorts make you buy more gear than the cable repair guy's got. It probably cost more than my first house.

DEXTER *(still trying to read)* As I explained, I need a hobby.

CHARLIE. Did your shrink also tell you there's nothing to be learned from mistakes you don't make yourself? You might as well have stayed home and had them send you a mess of fish by FedEx! Paying for fishing lessons or sex troubles my soul.

(DEXTER'S exasperated expression says "What a rude question!")

DEXTER. I've never paid for sex!

CHARLIE. Well, you paid for fishing lessons. Same thing.
\
DEXTER. Have you finished running me down? I don't even know you!

(DEXTER tries to hide in his magazine)

CHARLIE *(extending his hand)* We can fix that. Name's Charlie. You new around here?...Hey! You got a car?

DEXTER. Of course. Don't you?

CHARLIE. Sure, I got a car, but I'm not driving right now. Hey! I've got an idea.

DEXTER *(insulting)* You've. got. an. idea?

CHARLIE. Yeah. We go fishing! Together!

DEXTER. Why would I want to go fishing with you?

CHARLIE. You want to learn to fish and I'm an expert! We go out to the lake and drop a line or two? How about it?

DEXTER. Aw... I don't know...

CHARLIE. Your new hobby ...

DEXTER. My new hobby...

CHARLIE. You need ...

DEXTER. I need...what?

CHARLIE. To make your shrink happy?...

DEXTER *(considering this)* Make my shrink happy? Hmmm...

CHARLIE. Fishing lessons. Free.

DEXTER. Free, huh?

CHARLIE. I'll show you what real fishing is. I know just the spot.

DEXTER. Where?

CHARLIE. Successful fishermen never reveal their sources. How 'bout it?

DEXTER. Maybe...When?

CHARLIE. Saturday morning.

DEXTER. After breakfast?

CHARLIE. No, no, my God, no. If you aren't up at four, you ain't fishing correctly. You got to be out on the lake while it's still dark. You gotta be cold, hungry, utterly miserable. If the fish think you're comfortable, they sense weakness, and they will not bite. *(HE laughs)*

DEXTER. I don't want to miss my Saturday morning physical therapy session –

CHARLIE. You won't. We'll meet right here at four-thirty.

DEXTER. You don't mean a.m.!

CHARLIE. Four a.m.! Here's a reminder.

(*CHARLIE grabs DEXTER'S magazine and writes with a marker*)

CHARLIE. I'll bring the gear. You drive.

(*Charlie laughs to himself. DEXTER, resigned to going, exits.*)

CHARLIE. I could tell right away he's the kind who can't resist a bargain.

(*End of Scene I*)

Scene II – *At the lake.*

(*DEXTER and CHARLIE enter with fishing poles, two lawn chairs, a tackle box and a roll-on suitcase. CHARLIE opens the suitcase, removes two beers, hands one to DEXTER*)

DEXTER. Beer? At this hour? It's not even sun-up.

CHARLIE. Helps catch the worms.

DEXTER. We're going to fish with worms? Not flies?

CHARLIE. Worms. I used to have to dig for 'em. No more. Down in Florida, I learned to serenade them.

DEXTER. You sing to worms?

CHARLIE. Little-known fact: Worms have a discriminating taste in music. The music of the Earth. Drink your beer.

DEXTER. Before breakfast?

CHARLIE. It's necessary to get us some nice fresh worms. Drink.

> *(CHARLIE drinks. DEXTER shakes his head, reluctant)*

CHARLIE. You want to learn to fish? Drink it down to about half. Now.

> *(DEXTER drinks. CHARLIE digs in suitcase, pulls out two sandwiches, takes a bite, hands one to DEXTER)*

CHARLIE. I found it a good policy to eat before I fish. Otherwise, it tastes like bait.

DEXTER *(repelled)* This smells! What is it?

CHARLIE. Sardines for luck. Liverwurst for endurance. Jalapeños for courage. My pa swore by this combination, said it attracts the fish. Come on. Try it.

Now to find our bait. Did you know that beer amplifies sound? Basically, a half-empty beer can is like a metal detector for worms. Like this.

> *(CHARLIE gets down on the ground with his ear on the beer can)*

Come on! Help me! What are you waiting for?

> *(DEXTER reluctantly stoops, ear to beer can)*

CHARLIE. Hear them worms down there?

DEXTER. No.

CHARLIE. They're singin' their little hearts out. Over here. Listen.

(DEXTER crawls over to CHARLIE, puts his ear to his beer can)

DEXTER. I only hear the foam in the beer.

CHARLIE. There's a bunch of 'em down there, all right. We'll charm them buggers out of the ground with our saw music.

DEXTER. Saw music?

CHARLIE. Guys I know would pay thousands to learn this bait-catching technique. Here, I'm giving it to you for free...Yeah. First, I take a wooden dowel, like this.

(CHARLIE takes a wooden dowel and a hacksaw from suitcase)

Then I sink it down, about so far into the ground. Here. Try it! Like this. Then I take an old saw, rub the dowel real hard. Come on! Try it!

(CHARLIE hands another hacksaw and dowel to DEXTER. After a moment of disgust, DEXTER saws at the dowel)

CHARLIE. That's good. Underground, it sounds sort of like:

(CHARLIE makes a mouth sound, like a creaking door)

The worms think it's a mole. They get scared and rush to the surface where we scoop them up.

DEXTER. I'm supposed to believe that worms anticipate danger? That worms think?

CHARLIE. All creatures think. They think about what's in their best self-interest. Just like humans. It's survival! Figure out what the other guy thinks will give him an advantage – You don't really give it to him, you know, you just let the feller think he's gonna get it. Like what politicians do.

(CHARLIE closes the suitcase, sits on it, rubs the dowel with the saw)

Same with worms. Down in the Florida panhandle – the Redneck Riviera – they have an annual worm grunting contest. Actually, it's a big worm-grunting festival. Trophies. Big parade. A fancy ball where they crown a worm-grunting king and a worm-grunting queen. The whole shebang.

DEXTER. This is so bizarre I'm ready to believe it.

CHARLIE. I'll give 'em a few minutes to get agitated. We'll try for blue gills first.

DEXTER. I'm more interested in fly fishing. Trout.

CHARLIE. You're one of those elitists, huh? Here's how I see it. Salmon fishermen look down on trout fishermen. Trout fishermen look down on bait fishermen. Up north, everybody looks down on ice fishermen. Well, maybe it's carp fishermen at the bottom. Nobody wants to admit they eat carp. Carp will bite on anything. Marshmallows, paper plates, old political posters.

DEXTER. No matter how distasteful the candidate, I suppose.

CHARLIE. Hey! That's good! I wouldn't have taken you for a comedian! Elections are always rigged for the rich guy. I want a candidate like the All-American working-class panfish. They're dependable. Unlike what we got now. If panfish were underwear, they would be Fruit of the Loom. If they were beer, Pabst. If they were cars –

DEXTER. I get the idea. Ford. What do you drive?

CHARLIE. I'm not driving right now.

DEXTER. Trouble finding the bottom of the bottle?

CHARLIE. Let's not talk about it.

DEXTER. Next spring, I'm heading back up to Eagle River.

CHARLIE. For brook trout again? Sneaky things...

DEXTER *(patting the magazine)* "With unerring instincts..." says so right here.

CHARLIE. But stupid, I say...

DEXTER. Warrior personalities.

CHARLIE. Suspicious, paranoid creatures, lurking in dark holes. Just like the IRS.

DEXTER. "A trout who doesn't think like the fisherman is doomed for the frying pan." That's what my guide said.

CHARLIE. You hired a guide? Would you hire a valet to hang up your pants? Did you really hire a guide?

DEXTER. My first time fly fishing. Of course, I had a guide.

CHARLIE. That's highfalutin' fishing! Did the guide tie your flies on for you? Did he pull the fish in, too? What fun was that? I suppose he gutted them and fried them, too. What were you there for?

DEXTER. I wanted to learn to fish.

CHARLIE. Hiring a guide! That's like having a ghost-writer for your love letters. It's not natural! You might as well have stayed home and cleaned gutters....Here they come! Look! Aren't they beauties?

(Candy gummy worms appear on the ground)

DEXTER. The aesthetics of worms I have yet to appreciate.

(Eating his sandwich in one hand, CHARLIE proudly fingers worms with the other hand)

CHARLIE. Before we bait the hook, you got to spit on your worm. Here. Spit on this one.

DEXTER. *(much protesting)* Spit? No! No-no-no-no…No way!

CHARLIE. Sandwich saliva. My pa's secret weapon.

DEXTER *(resisting)* Uh-uh! No-no-no! Absolutely not!

CHARLIE. You want to catch fish, or not?

DEXTER *(resigned)* All right. Here goes.

(THEY BOTH spit on their worms and look at each other sheepishly)

CHARLIE. Now. Are we ready to fish?

DEXTER. Are you done messing with me?... In that case, I'm ready to fish!

(Lights down, to show passage of time)

SCENE III – Celebrating the Catch

(Lights up)

(With an arm on the other's shoulder, CHARLIE and DEXTER proudly hold a rope hung with a large catch of panfish. Smiling broadly, THEY pose for a photo)

(Lights: flash of a photo)

(Lights out)

END

ALL WASHED UP

Three Character Sketches
by Paullette MacDougal

TIME: The recent past.

PLACE: A laundry room in Marty's house.

CAST   *(Characters may be any ages relative to each other, and any races or ethnicities. Rosita is Spanish-speaking.)*

SCENE 1 – **ANGELA THE VIXEN**

ROSITA   Marty's wise and long-suffering housekeeper, cook, and domestic problem-solver, the only sensible person here.

ANGELA, WIFE #1   A new divorcee, Marty's Ex. She is slim, attractive, and obsessed with her image. She wears pretty underwear.

SCENE 2 – **HELEN'S MANIFESTO**

HELEN, WIFE #2   She's at the end of her rope. She's dressed for the office.

MARTY   Helen's husband. He's wears a towel.

SCENE 3 – **SALLY ANN'S GIRL SCOUTS**

MARTY   Rosita's serially single employer and Angela,
                    Helen's and Sally Ann's former husband.

ROSITA   Marty's housekeeper.

AUTHOR'S NOTE
(Each scene may be produced independently as desired)

SCENE #1 ANGELA THE VIXEN

by Paullette MacDougal

Domestic workers are rarely portrayed as indispensable heroines, which they often are. Rosita is one of these.

At rise: ROSITA enters with large laundry basket, speaks directly to audience.

ROSITA. Twenty years I've worked in this house. I clean, I cook, I do the laundry. Dirty clothes come in, clean clothes go out. I worked for all three of Mister Marty's wives right here. They come and they go, just like the laundry. *Ay, Dios mio.*

Folks think nothin' important happens here. *Nada?* Hah! This laundry room is the bull's eye, the H-Q, the belly button of the house! Here's where the real stuff happens, where promises come unglued, where the doh-doh hits the fan. No secrets hide from she who washes the clothes. Do you dare me to spill the suds?

Mister Marty's first wife was Missus Angela. What was it he called her?...Vixen? That's it! "The Vixen who has more clothes than Macy's." Don't tell anybody I told you...

> *(ROSITA exits, laughing)*
> *(Lights change)*

ANGELA *(off)* ROSITA! ROSITA! ROSITA! WHERE ARE YOU? ROSITA!

> *(ANGELA enters and frantically rummages through a clothes basket)*

ROSITA *(entering) Que pasa?* What happened?

ANGELA. Rosita, have you seen my new dress? The green one? We must find it.

ROSITA . You mean the one the top goes down to here...

> *(indicating a neckline down to her belly)*

And the bottom goes up to here. *No mucho* in-between?

> *(indicating a very short skirt almost up to her belly)*

ANGELA. Rosita! Don't be crude.

ROSTITA. *Un momento,* Missus.

> *(ROSITA exits. ANGELA continues her frantic search)*

ANGELA. Where, where? It's got to be here. Please, God, let it be here.

ROSITA *(entering)* It was in your closet.

> *(ROSITA produces the dress. ANGELA greets it like a dear friend)*

ANGELA. Oh, thank you, thank you, God, and Armani.

ROSITA. You're welcome. *(SHE exits)*

ANGELA. Of course. Thank you also, Rosita. Wait! Come back! I need to talk to you about –about your employment here.

ROSITA *(entering) Si,* Missus. What about my employment?

ANGELA. Since my divorce, money is tight, so I really don't need...

ROSITA. You don't need what?

ANGELA. I don't need your services any longer.

ROSITA. Maybe that will be true. We'll see. *(SHE almost exits)*

ANGELA. Wait. There's something else.

ROSITA *(wearily) Si*, Missus, just show me what all you want ironed.

ANGELA. You can call me Miss now, not Missus, Rosita. Today it's final. I'm single, single at last! And this is my first date! After all these years married to Marty Keller! I'm so nervous. Help me decide what to wear.

ROSITA. *Si,* Missus.

ANGELA. Miss.

ROSITA. *Si,* Miss.

ANGELA. Let's start with the Armani. Your honest opinion.

> *(ANGELA "models" the dress, by holding it in front of her)*

ROSITA. Looks okay, Miss.

ANGELA. Just okay? For a first date? A blind date, too. First impressions are so important, you know. Would you tilt that mirror a little to the left? The truth, now, Rosita.

ROSITA. It's nice, for what color it is.

ANGELA. And what color would you call it?

ROSITA. Dish rag green.

ANGELA. Washes me out, you mean?

ROSITA. *Si,* Miss.

> *(ANGELA tosses rejected dresses back to ROSITA, who hangs them back on the rack. ANGELA "models" a fire truck red dress)*

ANGELA. My Mama always said, "First looks tell."

ROSITA. My Mama always said, *Si una aguja puede pasarlo no lo quites con una hacha.*

ANGELA. What does that mean?

ROSITA. If a needle can pierce it, don't chop it with an axe.

> *(ANGELA reluctantly sheds the red one, takes a purple floral one)*

ANGELA. How about this one?

ROSITA. It talks too much.

ANGELA. You mean, I shouldn't appear too eager.

ROSITA. *Si,* Miss.

> *(ANGELA shutters and sheds the purple floral, takes the black one)*

ANGELA. Slenderizing.

ROSITA. *Me puse eso en un funeral.*

ANGELA. What did you say?

ROSITA. You're not looking for an undertaker.

> *(ANGELA sheds the black dress, takes another)*

ANGELA. My old standby. My go-everywhere dress.

ROSITA. We buried Aunt *Yurani* in one like that. She had the figure for it. *Muchas curvas. Grande* boobs. Tight ass.

(ANGELA sheds the dress like it's poisonous, takes another)

ANGELA. How about this? Honestly now.

ROSITA. Looks like you got it at a rummage sale.

ANGELA. I'll have you know this dress cost $800 at Saks.

ROSITA. You got robbed.

ANGELA. Rosita! I don't believe that's an appropriate response.

ROSITA. I give up!

(ROSITA exits)

ANGELA. ROSITA! Come back! You've got to help me! ROSITA!

(ANGELA pulls ROSITA back on stage)

ROSITA. Now what?

ANGELA. We haven't decided what I should wear yet.

ROSITA. Look at it this way. *Hombres* come in two kinds: The kind like women, the kind don't. The kind don't, don't matter. The kind do, they're not lookin' at the clothes. Their eyes are measurin' the body.

ANGELA. Please! My friend who arranged this introduction said my date is a fine gentleman.

ROSITA. *Hes el rico?*

ANGELA. You know I don't like words I don't understand. What did you say?

ROSITA. This *hombre,* is he rich?

ANGELA. It's rude to ask about one's wealth. She said he's charming, a prince of a fellow. That's what she said – a prince.

ROSITA. A prince, huh? Somebody still got to clean up after his horse. I got work to do.

(ROSITA starts to exit)

ANGELA. But what am I going to wear?

ROSITA. Come here. Close your eyes. Turn around three times...Now give me your hand.

(ROSITA guides ANGELA'S hand to the rack of dresses, praying) Virgen Maria, por favor ayudame, por favor ayudame, por favor ayudame.

ROSITA. *Perfecto! Buenisimo! Excelente!* That's the dress Holy Mother wants you to wear!

(ROSITA exits. ANGELA follows, waving the "dish-rag green" dress)

ANGELA. Rosita! This one's too tight! It washes me out! ROSITA! COME BACK! YOU CAN'T LEAVE ME WITHOUT A DECISION! ROSITA! I DON'T KNOW WHAT TO WEAR! HELP ME!

(Lights change to show passing of time)
(ROSITA enters, speaks to audience)

ROSITA. Miss Angela wore the too-tight, dishrag green dress, and galloped off into the sunset with her new color-blind prince to live happily ever after.

(ROSITA exits)

End, Scene #1

SCENE 2 - HELEN'S MANIFESTO

CAST: MARTY – Frustrated husband.
         HELEN – Marty's difficult second wife.
         ROSITA – Wise housekeeper, Latina.

(At rise: Rosita enters off side and addresses audience.)

ROSITA. Mister Marty's new Missus moved in. Real persnickety. Won't let me do her laundry.

(imitating Helen)

"Don't want nobody touching my unders."

(as herself)

The new Missus thinks Rosita knows *nada* 'bout laundry. So I quit. I did. I quit!

(ROSITA exits)
(Lights change)

(HELEN irons a pair of men's boxer shorts.
MARTY enters, wearing a towel.
HELEN ignores him and continues to iron)

MARTY. HELEN! #$$%^**!!!! I've got an early tee-off time, there's no breakfast and no shorts in my drawer. How much work is it for you to throw in a load of my underwear once a week?

HELEN *(mimicking him)* MARTY! $@$%^&**!!! I've got a breakfast meeting, there's no breakfast, and no panties. How much work is it for you to make your own breakfast?

MARTY. Helen, are you smarting off at me?

HELEN. Yes, Marty. I'm late for work. It was the quickie that made us late. Your choice. Quickie or punctuality. As usual, you chose quickie.

MARTY. Why are you standing there at the ironing board when you're in a hurry?

HELEN. This relaxes me.

> *(SHE holds a Sharpie pen. SHE has been writing on the shorts)*

MARTY. This relaxes you?

HELEN. It makes me not think.

MARTY. Isn't there just one pair of clean shorts around here?

> *(HE rummages through a clothes basket)*

HELEN. Those clothes are waiting to be ironed.

MARTY. How long since my son's worn this?

> *(HE holds up a small-sized boy's shirt)*

HELEN. Maybe he's ironing his own shirts now that he's at the University.

MARTY. What's this? A mouse's nest in the ironing basket! With five baby mice!

> *(HE holds up a mouse by the tail)*

HELEN. Put Mama Mouse back, please. The babies need her.

> *(MARTY rummages through another basket)*

HELEN. Those wet clothes are waiting to go into the dryer.

MARTY. What the hell's going on here? You on strike?

HELEN. You might call it that. Ever since you retired *(Or took that new position)*, you've expected me to wait on you 24/7.

MARTY. Aren't there any clean shorts, maybe just one pair of clean shorts, anywhere?

HELEN. Here's one.

MARTY. You're ironing my shorts? That's news. What the – This iron's not even plugged in!...There's writing on my shorts! What's going on?

HELEN. My manifesto.

MARTY. On my shorts?

HELEN. Read it.

MARTY. I need my glasses.

> *(HELEN hands him her glasses. HE reads from the Manifesto shorts)*

MARTY. "I, Helen, declare that I shall never again set foot into this laundry room. After careful consideration, instead of dousing it with kerosene and setting it aflame, I declare that I shall never coax one more spaghetti spot out of a white shirt, or bleach one more load of filthy white bath towels you've shammied the car with, or sanitize one more pair of smelly sports socks, or drag the big recycling bin full of beer cans out to the street every week. Furthermore..."
What the devil is this? I'm leaving. Without shorts.

> *(HE throws down the Manifesto shorts and exits)*

HELEN. You don't even want to talk about it?

MARTY. *(HE enters)* No, I don't! *(HE exits)*

HELEN. In that case –

> *(HELEN exits. MARTY re-enters, picks up the "Manifesto" shorts and exits. HELEN enters with two suitcases. SHE stuffs an armload of women's clothing from the soiled clothes basket into one. SHE stuffs an armful of wet, dripping women's clothing, into the other. MARTY enters, now dressed)*

MARTY. Why the devil are you putting wet clothes in a suitcase?

HELEN. Because, if I wait for them to dry, I might stay.

MARTY. Helen! Helen! Helen, let's talk. Helen!

HELEN. I asked you to discuss it on Sunday, Tuesday, and also this morning. Today was your last chance. You want me to make your meals, launder your clothes, pick up your wet towels, get your car washed. I can do all that. Now that I think of it, I have been doing all that. But I cannot be late for work. Goodbye, Marty.

> *(SHE heads for the door with both suitcases and exits)*

MARTY. Please, Helen…Give me another chance! Helen! Helen! HELEN! WAIT! HELEN! DON'T DO THIS TO ME! HELEN! WAIT! HELEN!

> *(MARTY exits after her, howling)*
> *(Sound: Car starting and leaving)*
> *(Lights: Change to show passage of time)*

ROSITA *(entering, to audience)* That's how that marriage went down the drain. For want of a good laundry lady.

> *(ROSITA exits)*

End, Scene 2

SCENE #3 – SALLY ANN'S GIRL SCOUTS

by Paullette MacDougal

CAST: ROSITA – Wise housekeeper. Latina.
MARTY – Frustrated almost ex-husband.

(Pre-set: A basket of women's clothing.
A box marked "GOODWILL."
`Makeup, hat, sun glasses, wig)

(At rise)

ROSITA *(to audience)* Then Mister Marty met Miss Sally Ann and they got married. I came back to work here again because she talked him into buying a beautiful new Maytag washer and dryer.

How Missus Sally Ann loved her Girl Scouts! That's how she got put in jail the first time. When Mister Marty coughed up money that time to bail her out, she celebrated by making popcorn for the whole neighborhood – in the clothes dryer! I liked Missus Sally Ann. Piety how it all turned out.

(Sound: phone ringing)
(Marty enters, very stressed. HE ignores phone, searching for absent Sally Ann, and barking orders)

MARTY. Dang it, Sally Ann, where are you? Rosita? Anybody here? SALLY ANN! SOMEBODY ANSWER THE PHONE! ROSITA! ANSWER THE PHONE! ROSITA! ROSITA! SALLY ANN! ANSWER THE DANGED PHONE!

(ROSITA enters hurriedly, answers phone)

ROSITA. *Hola...* Sally Ann! You okay, *mija?*...Okay. I'll see if he's here. If he is, he's all blown up like a toad. Why don't you let Mister cool down before you talk to him? You are where? *Dios mio*...That's a devilish trick, Sally Ann, a devilish trick. *(calling)* Mister Marty! Are you here? It's your latest Ex on the phone....MISTER MARTY? PHONE CALL!

> *(ROSITA calls, louder than she needs to, since MARTY stands right next to her. MARTY takes phone, his tone alternating between anger and whininess. ROSITA listens, pretending to be cleaning)*

MARTY *(very angry)* SALLY ANN? WHERE THE DEVIL ARE YOU? I'm here at the house to drive you to court. Are you at the courthouse already? You didn't drive, did you? With your license revoked? Sally, tell me you didn't drive...You took a cab? To the airport? The AIRPORT? WHATEVER FOR?...Of course you're going to court this morning! I put up $20,000 to get you out of the clink, and BY GOD, YOU'RE GOING TO SHOW UP, IF I HAVE TO DRAG YOU!...Yes, I imagine it would be embarrassing to appear in court, you "a highly respected political activist" and all...YOU'RE WHERE?

> *(unbelieving, then to ROSITA)*

She says she's on a plane to Las Vegas!

> *(to SALLY ANN on phone)*

Lay off the stupid jokes, Sally Ann! You're giving me another heart attack.

> *(to ROSITA)*

She says she was just helping out with the cookie sale.

> *(back to phone)*

Of course. Little Girl Scouts shouldn't be hauled off to jail! But you knew they're supposed to have a license to sell cookies in the mall... Sally Ann! You didn't have to hit the cop!

(to ROSITA, defeated)

She says her elbow got in the way of his nose...

(back to phone, HE sinks down to the floor)

You bit him, too? Why the hell?...

(to ROSITA)

She says she was defending the Girl Scouts.

(back to phone)

I thought they kicked you out as troop leader after the last incident! You, you what?...Kneed him in the – where? Sally Ann, get off the plane! Right now! We've got one hour to –

(SOUND: phone dial tone)

She hung up. Rosita! she hung up! Aaagghhh!

(MARTY, devastated, pounds on the floor)

Rosita! She's on a plane to Las Vegas and it's going to cost me $20,000, which I don't have, plus the loan shark – You know what those guys do to get their money? Concrete boots at the bottom of the river...Broken knees...fingernails pulled out...What am I going to do? Rosita, you gotta help me! Help me think of something! Think! Think!...Hey! You're about Sally Ann's size, aren't you? Yeah. You be Sally Ann, Rosita. You dress up in Sally Ann's clothes. We'll go down to the courthouse, and –

ROSITA. Not going to impersonate nobody, if that's what you're thinking.

MARTY. Gotta do something! We've only got an hour.

ROSITA. You got an hour. I got a house to clean.

MARTY. Rosita, you can't desert an old friend, can you?

ROSITA. Desert an old friend? You? *Si.* That I can do.

    (ROSITA turns to exit)

MARTY *(desperate)* Rosita, I beg you. Think of something. Please. Help me. Anything. I'll pay you. Anything. How about $500?

ROSITA. Five-hundred dollars? Well, on second thought, it wasn't a bad idea, actually, impersonating Sally Ann...Sure. It might work...

MARTY *(hugging her gratefully)* Rosita, my dear Rosita! I knew you'd help me.

ROSITA. You, not me.

MARTY. Me? What?...

ROSITA *(examining his face)* Did you shave real close today?...Might pass.

MARTY. Rosita! What are you doing?

    (ROSITA digs into box marked "Goodwill," finds a woman's dress)

ROSITA. You be Sally Ann. Here. This is before her last diet. Let's see how you look in this.

MARTY. No, no. I couldn't –

ROSITA. Okay. Don't then. I thought I heard you say, "anything." Guess you didn't mean it.

    (ROSITA starts to exit)

MARTY. Rosita, don't leave! You're right. I'll try anything. Help me. Please, Rosita, help me.

ROSITA. Five hundred dollars? *Claro que si.* First, write me a check. Five hundred smackers.

>*(SHE hands him his checkbook. Grumbling, MARTY writes a check as ROSITA digs in laundry basket. SHE finds panty hose or leggings)*

MARTY. You're a tough negotiator, Rosita.

ROSITA. Plus size. Might work. Now take off your pants.

MARTY. No, not those. Anything but –

ROSITA. You want my help, or not? It's this, or you let me shave your hairy legs.

MARTY. Okay, okay…Which end is up?

>*(MARTY, cussing under his breath, slips off his trousers and struggles to put the panty hose or leggings on over his shorts)*

ROSITA. Roll them up like this first…Carefully, carefully…You're gonna make holes! Stop! Let me help! …Like that. Pull them up. Carefully! There. That will have to do…Now. Take off your shirt! Here. See what you can do with this.

>*(ROSITA hands him a bra from the Goodwill box)*

MARTY. Not that! Please, not that!

ROSITA. It hooks together in the back. I think there's an old wig some place 'round here, left over from Sally Ann's *loco* stage.

>*(SHE exits)*

MARTY. They're all *loco* stages. *Esta mal de la cabeza.* What the #$%&*@!

> (*MARTY holds the bra like it's a rattlesnake. HE puts the bra on up-side-down, finally gets it right. It droops. ROSITA enters*)

ROSITA. Here's what you need.

> (*ROSITA adjusts the bra and stuffs two pair of socks into the cups*)

That's better...Now put on this dress. (*ROSITA exits*)

MARTY. ROSITA! Don't leave me! (*cussing, MARTY painfully finds his way into the dress,*)

ROSITA (*entering with high heeled shoes*) Good thing Sally Ann's got big feet. Try these on.

> (*HE tries to walk in the high heels, falls into a sprawl*)

ROSITA. Now a little color… (*SHE puts lipstick on MARTY*)

MARTY. Have some mercy, will you?

ROSITA. Keep practicing. Now say, "Yes your honor.."

MARTY. Yes, your honor.

ROSITA. No, no. Higher… and sexy…like Sally Ann.

MARTY (*in falsetto*) Yes, your honor.

ROSITA. Again. Three times. Keep at it.

MARTY (*in higher falsetto*) Yes, your honor. Yes, your honor. Yes, your honor. Yes –

ROSITA. Stop! That's enough! Tell you what, I'll even drive you – in your Beamer. I'll let you off right in front. If you have to walk from the parking lot, you might break something. Wait. Something's missing. Sally Ann never went anywhere without these. The finishing touch.

(ROSITA gives him a pair of gaudy sun glasses and sprays cologne)

MARTY (*HE sputters, coughs*) Isn't this going a little too far?

ROSITA. You wanna be Sally Ann, you gotta be Sally Ann like Sally Ann be Sally Ann. *Si!*

ROSITA. Now, wiggle your rear end like Sally Ann. *Un poco mejor. Perfecto! Buenisimo!* Mister Marty, you look goo-od! Might even work. Come along, Sally Ann. Baby, you goin' to meet the judge!

> *(MARTY painfully hobbles toward exit. ROSITA juggles the car keys, exiting)*
> *(Lights change to show passing of time)*
> *(ROSITA enters triumphantly. Still in high heels, MARTY enters painfully)*
> *(Offside, ROSITA speaks to audience as in beginning)*

ROSITA. He pulled it off! Mister Marty fooled the judge! Too bad Missus Sally Ann had to leave town before the next Girl Scout cookie sale. I wonder who will move in here next?...*No hay problema!* Like plumbing fixtures, curtain rods, and tenured professors, Rosita conveys!

> *(SHE surprises MARTY by kissing her hand and placing the kiss dramatically on Marty's cheek as she exits)*

END

LOVE ON ICE

A Romantic Comedy of a Frosty Passion
and a Peculiar Proposal
(Previous title: HOOK, LINE AND SINKER)

by Paullette MacDougal

CAST: *(Relative ages, 20s to 70s, any race or ethnicity)*

MARK#1:   A hearty eater who loves Cathy and ice fishing.

MARK#2:   Mark's secret thoughts about Cathy and ice fishing.

CATHY#1:   A high school English teacher who loves Mark and books.

CATHY#2:   Cathy's secret thoughts about Mark and ice fishing.

*(Spoken conversation between Cathy#1 and Mark#1 **in bold italics.**
Secret thoughts are spoken by Cathy#2 and Mark#2. Alternatively,
these may be pre-recorded for a two-hander)*

PLACE: On an ice-covered frozen lake in northern Minnesota.

TIME: In the dead of winter.

Acknowledgements

Thanks to Michael MacDougal and Cliff Morris for introducing us
to Brian Alberts, outdoorsman, fisherman, skier, and storyteller *par
excellence.* Alberts inspired this story.

Also, many thanks to actors Cathy Day and Mark Finn for their role
in the development of this short play and for inviting us to their comic
book-themed wedding, which was the real impetus for writing this story.

LOVE ON ICE

By Paullette MacDougal

SYNOPSIS

Mark has taken his long-time girlfriend Cathy out on the frozen lake to introduce her to his favorite sport, ice fishing, and to propose marriage. Cathy is not the out- door type. She prefers to be curled up in front of a warm fireplace, reading a book.

Mark's friend Johnny had convinced him to "do something unique and exciting, something you can brag about to your grandchildren." So Mark tied the diamond ring to the fish line and dropped it down through the hole in the ice. He fantasized that when Cathy pulls up her first catch (along with the diamond ring), it will not only be "unique, and exciting," but she will get "hooked" on ice fishing.

No chance. She's cold. She's bored.

And worse, the fish are not biting. But when a fish finally does bite, the ring is—where is the ring?

Honors

LOVE ON ICE (then entitled *Hook, Line, and Sinker*) was **Finalist** in **Dubuque (Iowa) Fine Arts Players National Playwriting Contest**

An earlier version of LOVE ON ICE was cited for **Honorable Mention (out of 18,000 entries), at Writers' Digest Competition.**

PARADOX PLAYERS, Austin, TX, premiered this play as part of a double bill of wintry, icy and snowy plays.

LOVE ON ICE

By Paullette MacDougal

LOVE ON ICE

By Paullette MacDougal

(Before curtain, SOUND of a cold wind)

(At rise, CATHY#1 and #2 and MARK#1 and #2 are heavily dressed for the deepest, coldest winter on a frozen Minnesota lake. They wait silently for a fish to bite.

Between them is a "fishing hole in the ice," topped with a facsimile of a a red-flagged ice fishing tip-up.

MARK#1 and MARK#2 are focused on the tip-up. THEY try, through pure will power, to entice a fish to bite. Cold and bored, both CATHYS shiver.

*MARK#1's AND CATHY#1's thoughts are spoken by MARK#2 and CATHY#2. Spoken conversation between Cathy#1 and Mark#1 is **in bold italics.**)*

(Sound: Wind fades)

CATHY#2: What am I doing here?

MARK#2: She's bored.

CATHY#2: I'd like to say something, but he said, "No talking." Supposedly, talking spooks the fish.

MARK#2: I should have known this wouldn't work.

CATHY#2: Are fish smart enough to be spooked?

MARK#2: Come on, fish, let's hurry this up.

CATHY#2: Why didn't I wear electric socks?

MARK#2: Last week the fish were practically leaping into my bucket. Tip-up, tip-up, tip-up – one right after another. I thought this was the same spot.

CATHY#2: I could be reading a book by my fireplace. Or doing the Sunday Crossword puzzle. Or staying in bed. With an electric blanket.

MARK#2: I think she's cold.

CATHY#2: I could be taking a hot bath.

MARK#2: This may have been a dumb idea.

CATHY#2: With bubbles.

MARK#2: If my truck hadn't fallen through the ice last year, we'd be snuggling up in my nice warm fishing shanty. If I'd parked that baby closer to shore, They could've towed them both out.

CATHY#2: Brrr. Must be thirty below zero.

MARK#2: My big, beautiful Chevy Silverado's still down there. Brand new battery, too. You could see the head lights through the ice for two days. Damn!

CATHY#2: I never thought I would rather be cleaning a bathroom…I think I'm catching a cold.

MARK#2: Come on, Fish, bite! Pop that little red flag will you? I can't wait to see her pull in her first catch, the thrill of her first strike –

CATHY#2: Probably pneumonia.

MARK#2: Then the surprise – her diamond ring! It was Johnny's idea. He's always coming up with stuff like that.

CATHY#2: Double pneumonia.

MARK#2: I hope I tied that ring on tight. More than I should've spent, but this lady's worth it. Oh! What if a big bass breaks the line and swims off with the ring? Why didn't I think of that?

CATHY#2: Now he's going to see me with a red nose.

MARK#2: I should've given it to her last summer when I took her out on the pontoon boat.

CATHY#2: Those shanties over there... Mark says some of them have bathrooms.

CATHY#1: *(speaking)* **Mark, I think I need to say someth–**

MARK#1: (speaking) **Shhh – You'll scare the fish away.**

> *(HE offers the thermos. CATHY#1 shakes her head)*

MARK#2: I thought she'd want some coffee to warm up.

CATHY#2: Coffee. Umm...But if I drink any, I'd have to – I'll try not to think about that.

MARK#2: My friend Georgie hid his girlfriend's ring under bandages and pretended he'd hurt his hand cutting hedges. His girlfriend wanted to help his change his bandage, of course –

> *(in "girlfriend's" voice)*

"Oooo, poor-Georgie, poor-Georgie." She fussed over him like he was half dead until she found the diamond safe and sound on Georgie's little finger. Yeah. I should've done that...Naw, the old bandage trick's been done already.

> *(mimicking Johnny's voice)*

"Gotta be unique, something we can laugh about later, like at your wedding reception." That's what Johnny said. So I tied a diamond ring tied onto a fish line! Very unique!...Very dumb!

CATHY#2: Some of the shanties over there have smoke coming out of the chimneys. Where there's smoke, there's – umm – warmth...

My cousin Janie, she's a nurse at the hospital in town. It's her theory that the big rash of babies born every November are conceived right out here on the lake. Janie said, "Something about ice fishing makes folks want to make babies. You and Mark need a warm shanty if you're going to make a baby out on the ice." Sure, Mark would still have a warm shanty if it hadn't fallen through the ice. With his truck. Dumb.

MARK#2: God, I miss my little shanty. Damn truck.

CATHY#2: Ten years. Maybe he doesn't love me.

MARK#2: Finicky fish. Maybe I used the wrong lure.

CATHY#2: If he really loved me, he wouldn't subject me to this. I ought to tell him, "Mark, at my age, I can't wait forever." Uh-uh. Must not bring up the subject of age. Plenty younger gals have their eye on Mark.

MARK#2: I should've taken her to the Eelpout Festival instead. Could've put the ring into her beer. Not very romantic, though. Eelpout! Ugly. Slimy. Nobody in their right mind admits they eat eelpout! French fried eelpout nuggets aren't so bad, though, if you drink enough.

CATHY#2: I could've married Wayne Mankowski 10 years ago. I hear his shanty has a bathroom, which I could use right now. Wayne's wife put an oriental rug in his shanty. Wayne went and cut a hole right in the middle of it – to fish through! I'd never marry a man who'd cut a hole in an Oriental rug!

MARK#2: Maybe I should've used a lighter line. Yeah. Number three Micro-Ice, maybe.

CATHY#2: Maybe Mark's just isn't the marrying type.

MARK#2: To some, ice fishing is a hobby. To me, it's a necessity.

CATHY#2: My sister said I've wasted ten years thinking Mark might be marriageable. Maybe she's right.

MARK#2: Not only lost my truck, lost all my gear, my auger, my flasher, my tip-up, my depth finder, even my underwater video camera. My whole arsenal – gone!

CATHY#2: How long can a gal wait?

MARK#2: If I had my underwater camera, I'd know if there really are any fish down there.

CATHY#2: Ten years I've waited. Geez!

MARK#2: Fishing blind like this gives the fish too much of an edge.

CATHY#2: But everybody says we're meant for each other.

MARK#2: A lady TV reporter come up from Los Angeles for the Eelpout Festival, saw all these little shanties. She said,

(imitating reporter's voice)

"I'm so sorry your little town is so poor."

I said, "What do you mean? We're not poor!"

She said, "All these shabby little houses. No trees. Looks poor to me!"

She didn't know she was standing on a lake! I had to auger a hole in the ice to prove it to her.

(BOTH MARK 1 and MARK#2: laugh)

That reporter gal high-tailed it back to shore as fast as her little high-heeled boots could carry her. Got to tell Cathy that one. She'd like that.

CATHY#2: I think he's laughing.

MARK#2: Poor? Who'd call us poor? Heck, we even have dances out here. And our annual Poker Run. I almost won the beard contest. Shaved it off when Cathy said I looked like a walrus.

CATHY#2: He is laughing. What could possibly be funny out here?

MARK#2: Poor! Huh! We're not poor! I mean the folks out here in Tip Up City got real houses in town, some of 'em pretty nice ones, too. So we're not poor – I mean the other folks aren't. Me, well, after my truck – Damn it all!

CATHY#2: I've never seen Mark change his mood so fast. Maybe he has a personality disorder.

MARK#2: Should've asked her before my truck fell in. Like right after the Polar Bear Plunge when she was warming me up in my old pickup. This gal sure knows how to turn on the heat!

CATHY#2: What's he thinking about now, with that sexy look in his eyes? I bet it's that new girl just moved in downstairs. Bleached blonde. Skinny as a rail except in two places, where she's too fat. Silicone, probably.

MARK#2: Why didn't I just give her the damn ring for her birthday? "Here, Cathy, let's get married." Gol'darn, if the ice had been thicker, we'd be cuddled up now, in my little old shanty, watching the tip-up from our bed.

CATHY#2: Mark said some of the shanties even have refrigerators. Refrigerators on an ice-covered lake? Isn't that redundant? I think my feet are frozen.

MARK#2: Dammit, Fish! Bite!

CATHY#2: He looks angry.

MARK#2: Maybe I should just pull up the line and call it a day.

CATHY#2: He is angry!

MARK#2: Sure. Just hand it to her: "Here's your cold, wet, slimy diamond ring." Very romantic. Wait until I get ahold of Johnny. "Ice on ice," he said. Him and his unique ideas!

CATHY#2: He's angry because I don't like this.

MARK#2: If I have to pull it up early, he'll be laughing at me for years.
:
CATHY#2: He can see I don't like this.

MARK#2: Screw Johnny! Two more minutes and I'm pulling up the line.

CATHY#2: If I stay with Mark, is this what I'll be doing for the rest of my life? Shivering on a frozen lake, watching a psychopathic maniac silently cussing at a hole in the ice?

MARK#2: Come on, Fish, save me!

CATHY#2: Maybe it's a good thing I discovered this side of him in time.

MARK#2: Some guys specialize, but I'll cook up anything that bites. An undersized crappie *(pronounced CRAH-pee),* or a stinkin' carp! Today, even an ugly single-whiskered eelpout!

MARK#1: *(whispers aloud to ice hole)* **Hey, Fish! Come on, little fishy, bite, will you?**

CATHY#2: I think he's talking to the fish.

MARK#2: Please, God, I never ask you to make the fish bite, but just this once?

CATHY#2: Angry creases between his eyebrows.

MARK#2: If you could please intervene and make a fish bite before some big ugly wide mouth comes along and steals the diamond?... Please, God. You know what a diamond costs these days?

CATHY#2: How he stares at the thing – what's it called? The tip over, flip up, something like that – like ice fishing is the most important thing is his life. More important than me, obviously.

MARK#2: Worse, if a fish steals this ring, Cathy will know what a fool I was for tying a diamond ring on a fish line...Geez, I love that woman.

CATHY#2: He's definitely angry at me. He wants me to pretend this is fun. It's not!

MARK#2: I'm going to kill Johnny!

CATHY#2: I'm not going to pretend, dammit!

MARK#2: No, I'll think of something worse than just killing him. I'll tie him up and put him in a barrel full of eelpout guts.

(MARK1 and MARK2 laugh)

MARK#2: That's what I'll do.

CATHY#2: He laughed! Sudden mood swings. I never noticed that before. Not a good sign.

MARK#2: Fish, if you don't bite right now – I'll – I'll –

> *(Suddenly alert as the RED FLAG pops up. There's a fish on line)*

MARK#1: Tip-up! STRIKE!

MARK#2: Now you got to handle this real careful. Give the fish twelve seconds to calm down.

MARK#1: and MARK#2: (*count "one-Mississippi, two-Mississippi, etc., under lines*)

CATHY#2: Something has happened. He's talking to himself...Maybe we can go home now.

CATHY#1: (*spoken*) **Mark, may I say someth—?**

MARK#1 (spoken) Shh – I got to concentrate...

MARK#2: Nine-Mississippi, ten-Mississippi, eleven-Mississippi. I'll let Cathy pull it in. She'd like that. Maybe even get hooked. Hooked? That's funny.

(*BOTH MARK#1: and Mark#2 are laughing*)

Like a new gambler who hits the jackpot. Hooked. That's a good one.

CATHY#2: He can laugh, but I can't talk.

MARK#1: Here, Cathy. Take the line.

(*Laughing, MARK motions to CATHY to hold the line. SHE resists*)

CATHY#2: What – ? He wants me to what? Hold a cold slimy fish line?

MARK#2: Maybe I should just pull it up myself and hand the damn ring to her. No, that would spoil the drama.

MARK#1: Hold it like this...

CATHY#2: *(hesitantly)* I guess I can do that. Not going to touch a fish, though. A slimy, flapping fish? No! No!!! Absolutely not! *(SHE stands, holds the line awkwardly at arms' length)*

MARK#2: Damn! She's gonna lose it. Felt like a big one, too.

CATHY#2: I don't like this. I hate this.

MARK#2: I can't stand it. I gotta help.

> *(MARK#1 puts his hand on line, guiding her movements)*

MARK#2: Hey! It is a big one!

CATHY#2: Why don't we just buy a fish at Safeway?

MARK #2: We don't want to lose this big fella!

MARK#1: Take it slow. Like this. Slow and easy.

> *(MARK#1, behind CATHY#1, hugs his arms around her, as he awkwardly guides her arm movements with the line)*

CATHY#2: Is this fun?

MARK#2: Now let the line play through your hand. God! It's a whopper! The Lochness Monster!

CATHY#2: Whatever he's doing, I don't get it.

MARK#2: Oh, my god! What if he's a wide-mouth buffalo head? He'd will break the line!

MARK#1: and MARK#2: *(unison)* **Easy now. Easy!** *Careful!*

> *(Some physical action here as MARK#1: manipulates the line himself)*

CATHY#2: What the hell is Mark doing?

MARK#2: Oh, my god! Oh, my god! He's gonna break the line! I'll be the laughing-stock of the whole county if he swims away with the ring! Cathy will be ashamed to be seen with me!

CATHY#2: Mark? Are you insane? This is not fun!

MARK#2: Calm yourself. Dad would say, "A little finessing. Give that baby a little finessing." Okay. Finessing. Just like Dad said. God, help me finesse!

(MARK#1 gives the fish line back to CATHY#1, speaking)

MARK#1: Here's the important part.

CATHY:#1 *(nervous)***The important part?**

MARK #1: Pull the line through your hand' til it's tight. That's it. Steady. Keep it up. Just like that. We're going to jerk the hook real sharp now. One-two-three!

(MARK#1 jerks the line. ALL FOUR look down the ice hole. MARK#1 and CATHY#1 speak aloud until otherwise indicated)

MARK#1: *(thunderous)* **Good one! Look-ee here, will you? Yah-hoo!**

MARK#1: Holy smokes! Look at the jowls on him!

(THEY pull up the fish, still on line, which "flaps" around in the "snow")

CATHY#1: Euugh!

MARK#1: Jackpot! A big one! Beginner's luck! He's huge! You did it, honey, you did it!

CATHY#1: Eh, this fish, what's it called?

MARK#1: (busy with the flapping fish) **Walleye.** *(Or Bass, Sturgeon, any local good catch)*

CATHY#1: (Walleye) is good, right?

MARK#1: (Walleye) is excellent. It's not only a (walleye), this might be the biggest (walleye) ever come out of Silver Lake! You caught the granddaddy of all (walleyes!) We'll take it to the game warden, get him measured official, get your picture taken for the newspaper! Hey! Your fish might set a record! We got to celebrate!

(*BOTH MARKS see that the ring is gone, go into panic mode*)

MARK#1 and MARK#2 (ad lib): **It's gone! Oh, God, it's gone! It's gone!**

CATHY#1: Mark, what's gone?

MARK#1: We let him play too long. We lost it! $@%&#+!*

MARK#2: You lost it. Don't blame me.

CATHY#1: Lost what? You got the fish out!

MARK#1: (angrily) **He got away with everything, hook, line, and** *(howling)* **RING!**

MARK#2: There goes my raise! $3000 bucks into the muck!

CATHY#1: Ring? I didn't hear a ring. I'll check the phone.

(*SHE takes a cell phone from her pocket*)

No message, either. Probably no signal, out here on the lake.

(MARK#1 wallops the fish with knife handle. BOTH CATHYS are horrified)

CATHY#1: Mark! What are you doing? You're hurting it!

MARK#1: No kidding!

(MARK curses under his breath, struggling with the "flapping fish.")

CATHY#1: Mark! You're so – so violent!

MARK#1: Right! I'm violent! Take that, thief!

(HE knocks the fish again. The fish's motion stops)

CATHY#2: I could never love a violent man!

CATHY#1: Mark, which way is the car? I'm going home.

CATHY#2: **Now I know why I send money to PETA. I can't stand violence to animals!**

(MARK#1 attacks the fish again, egged on by MARK#2. With knife, he starts to cut the head off. CATHY#1 and CATHY#2 scream)

MARK#1: Oh God, Oh God, Oh God! Let it be in here! Let it be in here!

(MARK#1: and MARK#2 have a prayerful panic as MARK cuts open the fish. Turning, so fish is out of sight, the actor exchanges"\whole fish" to pre-set "mangled fish." He throws gummy worm candy [fish guts] around)

CATHY#1: I want your car keys! I'm leaving! I need the your keys! Give me your car keys!

MARK#1: No, no. Wait! Wait! Wait a minute!

CATHY#1: Mark, give me your car keys! Or I'm going to walk home!

CATHY#2: I hate violent men…I hate …Mark! I think I hate you!

(MARK#1 sees CATHY#1 walking away)

MARK#1: Cathy! Don't go!

(looking up at her suddenly, MARK#1 cuts himself)

OUCH! Damn!

(Blood drips from MARK#1's hand)

Cathy! Wait! Just wait a min -- Ow! OOOO-Ow!

CATHY#1: Mark?...Mark?...Oh, you're hurt!

CATHY#2: Mark! My darling! Please don't bleed to death! What I would do without you?

CATHY#2: Mark! You're bleeding profusely! I've got to get you to a hospital!

MARK#1: Just a scratch. Most of the blood belongs to the fish.

*(*Mark#1 *keeps working on the fish.* Cathy#1 *offers her scarf)*

CATHY#2: Here – Let me wrap this around your hand.

MARK#1: (still working on the fish) Naw. Leave it be. A record catch is a big deal, no shit! We'll get a photograph in the newspaper. Got to have a photog—

CATHY#1: Photograph -- this?

MARK#1: Ehuu. Oh, shoot! Look what a mess. Oooooh!

MARK#2: Not much left to brag about.

MARK#1: It could have have been mounted, you know, to hang on the wall, if – damn!

> *(MARK#1 raises the mangled fish.)*

CATHY#2: Not very photogenic.

CATHY #1: I'M LEAVING!

MARK#1: Cathy! Wait! We can still take the pieces to the game warden, have them weighed, stick it back together and have it measured.

MARK#2: Let's skip the photograph.

MARK#1: Will you forgive me for messing up your trophy catch? I'll make it up to you. I promise you. Cathy, we can come ice fishing again some time.

CATHY#1: and CATHY#2: *(unison) No, thanks. (Both walk away)*

CATHY#2: Never!

MARK#2: Tell her you love her. Might be your last chance!

MARK#1: Oh, I forgot this part… I love you, Cathy.

CATHY#1: But I thought –

MARK#1: This isn't very romantic, but –

MARK#2: *Get down on your knees, you idiot!*

*MARK#1: (kneeling) **Oh, why is this so hard to say? Will you marry me? I'm sorry I don't have a ring for you, but Cathy, I want to marry you, but I wanted to give you a nice ring first –***

*CATHY#1: **Oh – oh- oh !***

> *(Fighting tears, CATHY#1 and* CATHY#2 *step away to have a private conversation. MARK#1 follows on his knees at a distance.)*

CATHY#2: Yippee! He finally said it!

CATHY#1: Yippee! Oh, I shouldn't have said that. It's childish.

CATHY#2: Say something mature, sophisticated, and intelligent…

CATHY#1: Like what? Something quotable?

CATHY#2: Something from Romeo and Juliet?

CATHY#1: If I could remember something quotable at a moment like this?

CATHY#2: You could say, "After all this time, you finally got around to asking me?"

CATHY#1: No, that might make him angry.

CATHY#2: How about, "Mark, I'm dying to marry you! Today! Let's get married today!"

CATHY#1: No, I don't want to sound too eager.

CATHY#2: No, you don't want to be too eager.

CATHY#1: I definitely don't want him to think I've been waiting ten years for him to ask…

CATHY#2: Just because you have been waiting ten years…

CATHY#1: *He looks so pitiful, like he's in pain. His knees must be frozen.*

CATHY#2: Maybe you should just say, "Yes?"

CATHY#1: *Just saying "Yes" sounds too – too – easy, or I mean, shouldn't there be some dialogue, like negotiation, or something memorable?*

MARK#1: *Cathy, say something!*

CATHY#1: *Eh - Eh –*

MARK#1: *(crushed) Cathy? You mean – You don't want to marry me? I love you so much. Let me explain about the ring. I promise, I'll buy you another ring, a bigger diamond, when –*

> *(CATHY reaches for MARK, squeezes his hand. MARK jumps from the pain)*

CATHY#1: *Mark. Mark. I – Oooo! I'm sorry! Poor honey! Is your hand hurting?*

MARK#1: *Naw. It's okay. About the ring…*

MARK#2: Keep talking! Tell her about the shanty.

MARK#1: *I'll build you the biggest, best-looking shanty on the lake, Satellite TV,*

MARK#2: The kitchen. Women love kitchens.

MARK#1: *A new stove – and a VitaMix!*

MARK#2: Tell her about the bed.

MARK#1: (excited) We'll have a nice warm bed – big enough for us both.

MARK#2: And the bathroom.

MARK#1: Even a bathroom. Yeah, a bathroom!

CATHY#2: I could use one right now!

MARK#2: She likes books.

MARK#1: (excited, blithering rapidly) Hey! And listen! I know you like books. Your books average fourteen point six seven five ounces each–

CATHY#1: Mark! What are you talking about? –

MARK#1: I weighed 'em –

CATHY#1: (interrupting) Stop! Stop right there. You weighed my books? Are you crazy?

MARK#1: All of 'em, which would put seven hundred pounds per square foot underneath – 'Way too much weight, so – so I figured I can build you two shelf units instead of one, kind of spread out the weight, you know, so you can bring all your books out on the lake without breaking the ice.

CATHY#1: (fumbling for words) Mark, I don't know how to say this.

MARK#1: You don't want to marry me? Don't say it then. Let's just pack up and go home.

(HE lays what's left of the mangled fish on upturned bucket)

CATHY#1: Mark, may I talk now? Mark?

MARK#1: Sure, Cathy. Talk all you want.

CATHY#1: Mark, I don't care if it's a big ring. Mark, I don't need – I don't care if it's not a big shanty. Little is okay.

MARK#1: (finally hearing her) **Really?**

CATHY#1: Big enough to stand up in? With a window?

MARK#1: Oh yeah. Big enough to stand up in. With big windows.,.

CATHY#1: (finding her own power) I don't care about big windows. But it's got to have a heater, if you want me to come back out on this lake! It's got to have a heater!!

MARK#1: Of course. A heater.

CATHY#1: Promise?

MARK#1: A great big propane heater!

CATHY#1: You promise for sure? A great big heater?

MARK#1: I promise. The biggest there is!

CATHY#1: A REALLY BIG HEATER! AND A BATHROOM! That's enough. I – I – if you promise.

MARK#1: I promise. A big heater and a bathroom.

CATHY#1: Then, I think, rather, I mean, no, I know – Of course, I want to – to – to marry you!

MARK#1: What? You do? You really do?...

CATHY#1:. I do. You see, I love you! Always have.

MARK#1: You have? You do? Oh, my God! Oh, my God! Oh, my —

(MARK jumps and runs about triumphantly...until he trips over some fishing gear, and falls. Down on the ice, he sees fish from a new angle. In a piece of the fish, HE finds the ring)

MARK#1: AAAAUK! Look! Oh – oh – oh! Look! Look! Oh, my god! Here it is! This is the best! Thank you. Thank you. Thank you.

(MARK#1 beats on the "ice" with his fists, howling)
(MARK#2 and CATHY#2 dance about)

CATHY#1 *(bewildered)* **You are thanking me? What for?**

MARK#1: Gods of the Lake, thank you! Oh, my god! Halleluiah!

(MARK#1 jumps about gymnastically, stomping the ice)

CATHY#1: Mark! Don't jump! You'll break the ice! We'll fall in! We'll die of hypothermia!

MARK#1: Gods of the Little Fishes that bite, thank you. Gods of the Little Fishes that don't bite, thank you. Gods of sunken trucks –

CATHY#1: Is this some bloody witchcraft fishing ritual? I thought you were Lutheran!

MARK#1: Here! Look!

(His hands still bloody, MARK offers her the ring)

CATHY#1: Oh! Oh! Oh. Oh. Ooooooo! Oh! I get it! This is why we went fishing?!

(Squealing with shock and recognition, SHE dissolves in laughter. HE places the rings on her finger, still attached to line, jig, tip-up, and red flag)

MARK#1: What do you think? It's not too small, too round, or something?

CATHY#1: It's perfect!

MARK#1: That's a relief. What shall we do to celebrate? Want to go to the Moose Tavern for a big steak?

CATHY#1: How about we skip the steak? Instead, let's do something really revolutionary with this fish.

MARK#1: Revolutionary? Like what?

CATHY#1: Like – cook it! It's already chunked up. Fish stew! With potatoes and carrots... Oh, Mark! I love you so much!

(MARK#1 and MARK#2 raise fists victoriously. CATHY 2 does cartwheels)

MARK#1 and MARK#2
MARK#1: Yah- hoo! STRI-I-I-KE!

> *(MARK#1 kisses CATHY#1 passionately. The hook, line, red flag, tip-up, and what's left of the mangled fish are dragging from her hand. The two conspirators, MARK#2 and CATHY#2, high-five, Jitterbug, twirl, or cheer-lead, and hug triumphantly)*

END

Have fun, and don't get "frost-bit."
— *Paullette MacDougal*

PRODUCTION NOTES for LOVE ON ICE

SET: *Ice covered with "snow" (fleecy king-sized blankets) with approximation of ice fishing apparatus (a "jig") sticking out. To be "authentic," actors sit on over-turned plastic paint cans.*

COSTUMES: *All wear jackets, scarves, mittens, boots.*

PROPS: *Two false fish. One is whole, one mangled, any large species.*
A "tip-up" or jig with a red flag.
Gummy candy worms make good "fish guts."

CPSIA information can be obtained
at www.ICGtesting.com
Printed in the USA
BVHW030502211020
591456BV00001B/2